Prophecy, Populism, and Propaganda
in the 'Octavia'

OPUSCULA GRAECOLATINA
(Supplementa Musei Tusculani)
Edenda curavit Ivan Boserup

Vol. 25

Patrick Kragelund

Prophecy, Populism, and Propaganda in the 'Octavia'

MUSEUM TUSCULANUM PRESS
COPENHAGEN 1982

© Museum Tusculanum Press
Printed in Special-Trykkeriet Viborg a-s
ISBN 8788073130
ISSN 0107-8089

Contents

Acknowledgements	6
Preface	7
I.1 The ambiguities in Poppaea's dream narrative	9
I.2 The interpretation suggested by Poppaea's nurse	15
II.1 The *thalamus* and the sword	22
II.2 "Victoria populi Romani"	38
Epilogue	53
Appendix I-III	55
Manuscripts, editions, translations, and literature referred to	62
Notes	71

Acknowledgements

This book has been long in the making, and in the process I have incurred depts of gratitude towards a great number of individuals and institutions. My interest in the subject goes back to a winter-term 1976-77 spent at the *Albert-Ludwigs-Universität* in Freiburg in Br. I am indepted to the late prof. dr. Karl Büchner for much advice, criticism and encouragement at that initial stage. The investigations were pursued at the University of Copenhagen and, in the winter 1980-81, at the Danish Academy in Rome. I have had the opportunity of presenting and discussing some of the results at a meeting of the *Filologisk Historiske Samfund* and at seminars at the Classical Department here in Copenhagen. At various stages of my work I have received grants from the following institutions: The *University of Copenhagen, Dronning Ingrids Romerske Fond* and the *Danish Research Council for the Humanities;* the Research Council has furthermore defrayed the cost of printing the book.

Among those who have generously given me their help, criticism, and advice are Bo Alkjær, Jerker Blomquist, Peter Lambert, Lars Mortensen, Marianne Pade, Erik Petersen, and Ole Langwitz Smith at the Copenhagen Classical Department, Tønnes Bekker-Nielsen, and Ole Thomsen at *Aarhus University,* and Anne Kromann Balling at the *Royal Collection of Coins and Medals.* Ivan Boserup and Kristian Jensen have followed my work over the years; at a critical juncture Johnny Christensen, Karsten Friis-Jensen, and Minna Skafte Jensen went over the whole manuscript with me. Marianne Alenius has read all the succeeding drafts; I have drawn heavily on her knowledge of Senecan scholarship; in my search for a plausible historical context for this play her criticism has had great impact.

To write in a language not one's own is a Procrustean experience. If the result is less so for the reader, the credit should go to M. A. Suzanne Dixon, now at the *Australian National University;* at the final stage she revised and improved the language of the book; in her congenial and inspiring manner she also suggested a number of important alterations.

Copenhagen, September 1982

...in our zealous haste towards the goal of our knowledge we may overlook the means of knowledge – language itself. The danger is a real one because it is in the nature of language to be overlooked, to be a means and not an end, and it is only by artifice that the search-light can be directed on the means of knowledge itself.

Louis Hjelmslev. *Prolegomena* p. 2.

Preface

The *Octavia* was transmitted to posterity among the tragedies ascribed to Seneca, but has generally been assigned to a later date. Arguments against Seneca's authorship have been based on internal evidence, a discrepancy in the manuscript tradition, and on stylistic grounds. The play is now generally – and, in my opinion, correctly – considered non-Senecan.

This uniform conclusion has been reached by scholars who argued from different categories of evidence, but were apparently unanimous in the assumption that the only aspect of the *Octavia* worthy of discussion was the question of its authenticity.[1] The tendency to treat the play as an appendix to its lost titlepage has, in my view, kept the discussion on unproductive lines by diverting attention from its content.

This misplaced emphasis is evident in the treatment of one of the finest – and most enigmatic – scenes of the play: that in which the empress Poppaea recounts to her nurse the dream she had on her wedding night (690ff). This passage has received more scholarly attention than almost any other in the play – not because of the obscurity of its function or meaning, but because it seems to contain a number of anachronisms which might enable the scholar to determine the provenance of the work. Scholars have, therefore, been tempted to suspend their interpretative skills on sighting references which *ex evenlu* established some point of fact, disregarding the greater part of the dream's content in their search for historic detail which would help them to determine whether the author knew Nero's actual fate.

It will, in fact, be argued that internal evidence not only suggests a post - Neronian date, but throws some light on the ideological stance of the author and, by implication, on the purpose of the play. At the same time, I shall attempt to correct what I see as an imbalance in the traditional preoccupation with the issue of whether Poppaea's dream represents a *vaticinium ex eventu*. This preoccupation has too often led scholars to overlook the more profitable course of establishing what such a *vaticinium* means qua *vaticinium,* and the significance and function of this particular *vaticinium* in the *Octavia.* Far from being self-evident, its significance emerges only from an analysis and "decoding" of the symbolic language employed in the dream scenes found in Roman literature. My discussion of dreams in Vergil represented one such attempt.[2] Using similar techniques, I shall offer an interpretation which, leaving aside the question of *who* wrote the play, will (I hope) improve our understanding of *what* he wrote.

The analysis provided here will throw new light not only on the dream of Poppaea but also that of Octavia. In the symmetrical structure of the play, the contrast between these two dream scenes is, as we shall see, of crucial importance. It will, however, be necessary first to deal almost exclusively with Poppaea's dream narrative and the various attempts to solve the riddles of that scene: like the riddles of the sphinx, they are the key to the rest.

I. 1. The ambiguities in Poppaea's dream narrative

The dreams described in Roman literature have a remarkably stable and uniform repertory of signs. The *appearance* of a person and the *items* and *actions* described in such dreams are part of the message about future events conveyed to the dreamer. In the dreams commonly termed symbolic, such features are in fact the only means of communication employed. The comments of scholiasts, the comparison with analogous scenes, and the dream scenes themselves render the meaning of these signs reasonably certain. Furies[3] and pale,[4] wounded,[5] sad or mourning[6] figures normally have a sinister significance; darkness,[7] flames,[8] torches,[9] dirt,[10] blood,[11] fear,[12] solitude[13] and falling[14] are likewise signs of misfortune. The repertory of favourable signs is, for obvious reasons, less extensive. Most of the signs are simple antonyms – as, for instance, light,[15] beauty,[16] and ascending.[17]

This repertory of signs may be regarded as a social system of communication comparable to gesture and ritual and seems to have been as commonplace to a Roman author, playwright or audience as certain acoustic and visual symbols in the movies are to us. It was employed primarily in the "higher" literary genres. Though not the first to employ the conventions – the tradition can be traced to earlier authors[18] and there are indications that staged dream scenes used the same symbolic scheme – Vergil appears to have given them their classic form. Our purpose is to determine how a Roman audience of the period understood the conventions.

Poppaea's dream falls into the symbolic category. In it, she saw a perverted celebration of her wedding with Nero: a crowd of women with hair unbound were lamenting her fate. At the sound of *tubae*, her husband's mother came forth, blood-stained torch in hand:

"...Visa nam thalamos meos
celebrare turba est maesta: resolutis comis
matres Latinae flebiles planctus dabant;

> inter tubarum saepe terribilem sonum
> sparsam cruore coniugis genetrix mei
> vultu minaci saeva quatiebat facem." (718 ff.)

In other words, she saw a Roman funeral. The wailing women, the tuba and the torch all belong to such an occasion. As so often in such a context, a torch-bearing fury – in this case embodied in Agrippina – appeared and dragged Poppaea along with her. Suddenly the earth opened before Poppaea's feet and she fell, head foremost, into the infernal regions.

> "Quam dum sequor coacta praesenti metu,
> diducta subito patuit ingenti mihi
> tellus hiatu; lata quo praeceps..." (724ff)

In dreams described in Roman literature furies, torches, and blood are, as we have seen, normally signs of misfortune.[19] Taken together with the funeral ceremonial,[20] these visions therefore seem to predict that Poppaea's marriage to Nero would result inher death. In fact, she appears to have witnessed her own descent into Hades: the fury forced[21] the frightened[22] empress to follow and she fell[23] into the gaping abyss[24] from which furies and ghosts emerged.[25]

It has been argued that nothing in this dream presupposes the author's knowledge of the manner or timing of Poppaea's death. This is strictly true, but the argument overlooks the limitations imposed by literary convention on the style of a *vaticinium*. Admittedly, it would not be possible to deduce from these visions the fact that Poppaea died because a kick from Nero induced a fatal miscarriage, but this is simply not the kind of information to be expected of a dream described in Roman literature. There are several reasons for this. One lies in the rather limited range of possibilities of a symbolic language such as is found in dreams of this type. Even if we add the signs of augury and folkloric features like funeral ceremonial, the restricted repertoire and structural properties of the signs in this code did not enable the author to describe exactly what was going to happen. Nor would this be regarded as likely, from a religious or philosophical point of view. The gods were not expected to speak in any but vague and general terms about the future.

Among the conventional signs in the second half of Poppaea's dream there are, nonetheless, features which, according to numerous scholars, imply that the author (and audience) knew exactly what was going to happen:

"...lata quo praeceps toros
cerno iugales pariter et miror meos,
in quis residi fessa. Venientem intuor
comitante turba coniugem quondam meum
natumque; properat petere complexus meos
Crispinus, intermissa libare oscula:
irrupit intra tecta cum trepidus mea
ensemque iugulo condidit saevum Nero." (726ff.)

To her astonishment, Poppaea found her marriage bed in Hell. Feeling tired, she sat down. Her former husband, Crispinus, followed by their child and his friends, entered and kissed her. A terrified Nero then rushed in and thrust a sword into his throat.

Poppaea then awoke. What worried her about this dream – so she told her nurse – was seeing her husband wounded. Her concern was justified: this was the most common way in which to announce a person's death in dreams of this type.[26]

We are, however, faced at this stage with the rather curious problem that we are left in doubt as to whether Nero has cut Crispinus' throat or his own. Poppaea's narrative is ambiguous on this point: *iugulo* stands unspecified, with nothing to tell us to whom it belongs. Nor is it clear to whom Poppaea is referring when she asks why she had seen her husband's blood:[27] she calls both *coniunx*(722;729).

The problem has been much debated.[28] Some of those who hold that Crispinus is the one being wounded[29] have regarded this as an argument in favour of Seneca's authorship. Crispinus – so runs the argument – was not killed by Nero, but forced to commit suicide in A.D. 66,[30] a fact of which the dream betrays no knowledge.

As I have pointed out, this type of argument is based on the false assumption that these dreams necessarily *depict* what is going to happen: an assumption I term the "realistic fallacy". If Crispinus is the one being wounded, this is first and foremost a conventional sign which tells us that he is going to die. Even if the author knew what actually happened to Crispinus (as he probably did) he would be expected to indicate it only in a vague and indirect manner. Those who opt for Nero have also failed to realize this. Even the fact that Nero did actually cut his own throat[31] is far from being conclusive – for two reasons. It *might* be a coincidence: many Romans died in that way and some even dreamt about it.[32] What is more important, the fact that this dream seems to allude to Nero's actual manner of death still fails to explain the striking ambiguities in Poppaea's narrative. The investigation needs to be taken further.

It is illuminating at this point to compare Poppaea's dream with that of Octavia in the beginning af the play (115ff): Octavia tells her nurse that the shade of her brother Britannicus appears before her, night after night, bearing torches. He tries to exact revenge on Nero, but fails. Terrified, he flees and seeks protection in his sister's arms, but Nero drives his sword through them both. In the language of their kind, both of these dreams predict the death of the person wounded, and in some respects the action in these dreams follows a similar pattern: Nero rushes into his wife's bedroom and kills somebody with his sword. We shall examine these similarities more closely in the second section. Here it must suffice to point out that some of them seem to indicate that Crispinus is the one who is being killed. What seems to point in the same direction is the description of Nero's sword as *saevum*.[33] There are, however, features which point in the opposite direction. In Octavia's dream, Britannicus was said to be terrified (*trepidus* 120), not surprisingly, as he tried to escape the armed Nero, but in Poppaea's dream the armed Nero – not, as might be expected, Crispinus – is the one who is terrified (*trepidus* 732). Nero's role in this dream corresponds more nearly with that of Britannicus in Octavia's dream – and to judge from various other dream parallels, Nero's fear portends some personal misfortune.[34]

The evidence thus seems to point in two directions at once and it is apparently a matter of (somewhat arbitrary) choice whether one argues that Nero's being armed *and* terrified indicates that he is going to kill – or to be killed. The majority of scholars have made a choice, but it is noteworthy that some expressed strong doubts when doing so,[35] while others decided in favour of one view but later reversed their decision. Thus Ladek originally was ambiguous, but later he settled for Nero.[36] Münscher held that Nero cuts Crispinus' throat in 733, but changed his mind within the year, to argue that Nero was here committing suicide.[37]

The translations of the *Octavia* reveal the same uncertainty: according to Nuce, Brisset, Nini, Linage, Marolles, Greslou, Stahr, Bradshaw, Gustafsson, Miller, Ageno, Mignon, and Paratore Nero was killing Crispinus; but according to Dolce, Swoboda, Desforges, and Herrmann he was committing suicide.[38] This also seems to be the import of Thomann's translation, although in his index af proper names he vacillates, to the reader's confusion.[39] Watling has taken the wiser course of reproducing the ambiguities, thus passing the problem on to his readers.[40]

This calls for caution. It would be mere guesswork to assign the token of misfortune (the wound) to either of these men as long as the text seems to relate it to both of them indiscriminately.

How, then are we to explain these lines? In my view, one of the curious things about the lines is that they seem to be ambiguous wherever they *could* have supplied a simple answer to the question: whose throat did Nero cut and, consequently, to whom is the sign of misfortune related? That *iugulo* (733) stands unspecified is in itself arresting, in an author who abounds in pronouns and possessives.[41] In the dream alone, we find *thalamos meos* (718), *coniugis ... mei* (722), *toros/ ... meos* (726-7), *coniugem ... meum* (729), *complexus meos* (730), *tecta ... mea* (732), and then suddenly just *iugulo* where a *suo* or *eius* could have settled the matter. To which of the two is Poppaea referring? Why, in any case, use an ambiguous expression like *coniugis* (739) where a name or other specification could have made it clear which man's death the dream is predicting?

When we try to solve this problem we should keep in mind that in antiquity the person who recounted a dream was regarded almost as a medium: the words and visions to which he lent his tongue were not wholly his own, but were conceived as messages in a foreign tongue or as lines in a cryptic poet. Cicero accordingly compared the interpretation of dreams to the translation of messages from Spanish envoys in the Senate – or to scholarly interpretation af poetry.[42] It is because of this *nomen omen* belief that puns, numerals and ambiguities[43] in oracular language were recognized as proper means of communicating.

Until now I have primarily translated the conventional signs found in Poppaea's dream. This approach has provided us with an answer to the questions with which Poppaea concludes her narrative of this cryptic dream:

"Heu quid minantur inferum manes mihi
aut quem cruorem coniugis vidi mei?" (738-9)

To judge from these questions, Poppaea felt that her dream had two messages: one which dealt with her own fate and one which dealt with that of her husband. Accordingly, she asks what the visions of Agrippina's *threatening ghost* foretold would happen to herself and what it meant that she had seen her husband's *blood* – these being the two most sinister signs in her dream.[44]

We know what these signs mean in dreams of this type: they predict the death of Poppaea and of her "husband" (Nero/Crispinus). All three died after Seneca: Poppaea in 65, Crispinus in 66, and Nero in 68. If the only point at issue is that of authorship, it is purely a matter of establishing that these *vaticinia* were, or were not, *ex eventu*. If our aim is to understand the play, the problem is more complex. It becomes necessary to address ourselves to the question of *why* the author left room for uncertainty in the matter of the wound: what was the general significance of such ambiguity in dreams of this sort and why, in this particular case, is Poppaea's account consistently ambiguous about "her husband's" ominous wound?

In order to answer this question, it is necessary to examine the interpretation of the dream which Poppaea's nurse offers.

I. 2. The interpretation suggested by Poppaea's nurse

The nurse's interpretation falls into six parts. She first presents some general reflections on the nature of dreams (740-2), then argues that it is only natural that Poppaea should have dreamt about *husband, wedding* and *bed* while lying in Nero's arms (742-4). As we shall see, this is an explanation of the dream as a whole: the features discussed occur at the end, beginning and middle of Poppaea's narrative.[45] The nurse then changes course, to discuss various features in the order in which they had occurred in the dream:[46] the significance of her seeing a *mourning crowd* of women (744-7), a *torch* in Agrippina's hand (748-50), her *bed* in Hades (750-1), and, finally, the *armed Nero* (752-3).

Yet from what we know of Roman divination the nurse's interpretation is false from beginning to end. It represents a rather forced attempt to convince Poppaea that her sinister dream is actually favourable. The nurse omits, distorts, and misinterprets every possible element of the dream in order to convince Poppaea that a glorious future awaits Nero and herself. In vain. Poppaea is clearly far from being convinced: she intends to sacrifice and to pray to the gods to divert their anger to her enemies. The scene closes with the empress asking her nurse to pray for the preservation of the *status quo*.

It will become apparent that the importance of the nurse's reply does not lie in its effect on Poppaea. Its function is, rather, to throw into relief Poppaea's terror and the ghastly prospects of her dream while reflecting the worries of the faithful nurse and her vain strivings to give the whole thing a less unfavourable aspect. We shall now examine the means she employs.

Her first point, that it is only natural Poppaea should dream of husband, wedding and bed while lying in Nero's arms, takes us back to the problem we set out to solve: how does the nurse account for the fact that what Poppaea says about her husband in l. 732ff is ambiguous? It emerges, in fact, that she *reproduces* these ambiguities:

"...Coniugem, thalamos, toros
vidisse te miraris amplexu novi
haerens mariti?" (742-4)

The word *coniunx* is here employed quite as ambiguously as in Poppaea's questions (739). Is it Nero or Crispinus she dreamt about while lying in Nero's arms?

According to Nordmeyer, *coniugem* refers to Crispinus, *novi ... mariti* to Nero.[47] Yet, as we have seen, the nurse is here offering an interpretation of the dream as a whole: she explains it as natural in the circumstances. Since Poppaea was lying in *Nero's* arms, how can it be certain that *coniunx* refers solely to Crispinus?

Helm took the opposing view, arguing that the nurse meant Nero when she said *coniugem*.[48] Why, then, did she not say so? If she meant Nero exclusively, why repeat Poppaea's ambiguous expression? And why interpret the dream as if Poppaea had dreamed of only one of them? She had, after all, dreamed of Nero *and* Crispinus.

To me, the true problem of these lines is of a different kind. Why is the nurse so ambiguous on this point *that one would hardly guess Crispinus had appeared in the dream at all, if Poppaea had not said so herself?* In my opinion, her ambiguity is deliberate. It is a device to make the dream appear less unfavourable to Poppaea. It enables her to acknowledge what she could not deny, that Poppaea dreamed about Nero *and* Crispinus, without having to explain this disquieting fact in terms of an interpretation. As she has said, there is, after all, nothing strange in dreaming about husband, wedding and bed on a wedding night!

The nurse refrains, furthermore, from interpreting the equally disquieting fact that Poppaea saw a crowd of women celebrating her wedding as a funeral. She offers, instead, a seemingly natural explanation: they were actually lamenting the fate of Octavia. She does, however, pass on to interpretation – if that is the word for it – in the following lines. The menacing fury, Agrippina (the nurse euphemistically speaks of the *Augusta*) had appeared in the dream with a blood-stained torch in her hand. As demonstrated above, such a torch is in all analogous instances on record a sign of death and disaster. The nurse, however, pretends it was a wedding torch[49] and regards it as a sign of the "illustrious name"[50] which Poppaea should win for herself! By the nurse's account, what is more, Poppaea's wedding bed could not have been situated in a more promising place than Hades, for in this the nurse discerns a guarantee that Poppaea's union with the eternal imperial House would prove to be well consolidated.

In Poppaea's narrative Nero killed somebody with his sword. The nurse interprets this sign of misfortune in her own way:

"Iugulo quod ensem condidit princeps tuus:
bella haud movebit, pace sed ferrum teget." (752-3)

Again, she reproduces one of Poppaea's ambiguous expressions: is *iugulo* the throat of Nero or of Crispinus? As the nurse does not mention Crispinus in this context, it has been argued that this can only be Nero's throat. The fact remains that Poppaea had actually dreamed of Crispinus as well, though the nurse consistently avoids mentioning this. The true problem of these lines is, therefore, not whether the nurse is alluding to Nero or to Crispinus exclusively, but why she persists in the ambiguity. In my view, her ambiguity is also here a means of making the dream appear less unfavourable. Characteristically, the nurse takes advantage of the expression used by Poppaea to describe Nero's murderous actions: according to her, Nero was actually sheathing his sword – *ensem condidit* can have this non-violent meaning – and with this peaceful gesture inaugurating a period of Augustan peace. It is equally symptomatic that in her rendering the throat is divorced from its original context. She speaks as if it were some object in which Nero had sheathed his sword peacefully and without bloodshed.

The patent absurdity of these interpretations is explicable: the nurse's task is more or less hopeless. She cannot omit or distort *everything* Poppaea has told her. Even if we did not know what Poppaea had actually dreamed it does not sound convincing that a marriage bed in Hades is a propitious sign or that a man who sheathes his sword in this way has peaceful intentions. No wonder, therefore, that her optimistic interpretation fails to convince Poppaea. Notwithstanding, it cannot be discounted as irrelevant to our interpretation of Poppaea's dream. Her very style of omission and distortion emphasizes what it is that makes this dream so disturbing to a Roman: the sinister prospects of Poppaea and "her husband".

This leaves us with the task of providing an explanation which accounts for these ambiguities. Let us first consider the suggestion of Fuchs, who seems to regard them as due to a lacuna between 738 and 739.[51] I think this highly unlikely. The dream scene is designed symmetrically: the dream narrative and the interpretation have the same number of verses. The dream narrative is, moreover, placed in the centre of the dream scene, with twenty-eight verses on either side:

Nurse	(690-711)	22		} 28
Poppaea	(712-739)	28	⎧ 6 ⎫ ⎨ 16 – DREAM NARRATIVE ⎬ ⎩ 6 ⎭	
Nurse	(740-755)	16	– INTERPRETATION	} 28
Poppaea	(756-761)	6		

The same tendency is observable in three other scenes of the play,* so there is nothing to support a solution such as that of Fuchs.

Thomas has an alternative explanation. He argued that the text as it stands is hopelessly ambiguous.[52] He therefore advocated reconsidering the emendations of Lipsius and Raphelengius: Lipsius[53] suggested the reading *tuo* (*sc. iugulo*) in place of *tuus*. His pupil Raphelengius[54] accordingly altered *mea* to *meo* (*sc. iugulo*) in l. 732 – with the result that Poppaea becomes the one whose throat is cut!

Thomas did not have access to Lipsius' *Animadversiones* and relied on Hosius' edition in which Lipsius' *tuo* is said to have been founded on *codicum deteriorum unus aut aliquot*.[55] I have found nothing to support Hosius' view – Lipsius' suggestion seems to have been purely conjectural. In the sixteenth and seventeenth centuries a number of scholars tried in this way to make sense of

---

* Cf. the appendix on symmetry in the *Octavia* p. 54ff.

these ambiguous lines: thus Lipsius suggested *meus* – not *meo*, as Raphelengius would have it – for *mea* in 1.732.[56] Delrio was prepared to accept this "if it had any manuscript authority" (*mallem 'meus', si quis liber confirmaret*),[57] whereas Gruterus[58] thought *meo* preferable *si vox ultima reformanda esset*. His own inclination was to substitute *Nero* for *mea* in 1.732 and *meo* for *Nero* in 733. Raphelengius accepted Lipsius' *tuo* for 1. 752, but termed it a "bold conjecture" (*corrigo audacter*).[59] Gruterus did not reject Lipsius' suggestion, but had some reservations about it.[60]

None of these emendations has been incorporated in the editions of the *Octavia*: the discussion has been confined to the *Animadversiones* and *Notae* of the scholars.[61] Indeed, Gronovius' objections seem to have put an end to the discussion as early as 1661.

Before we review Gronovius' objections to this approach we should perhaps acknowledge that the solution, neat and elegant as it is, clarifies the ambiguity of the text in only two of the five instances in which we are in doubt as to whether Nero or Crispinus is alluded to:

1. In the dream, Nero's terror and his armed state seem to indicate that he was going both to kill and to be killed (732-3).

2. and 3. In l. 733, the language leaves us uncertain into whose throat Nero thrust his sword – as is the case in the line quoted above (752).

4 and 5. Nor are we told to which of her husbands Poppaea was referring in 1.739 and which of them the nurse meant in 1.742.

Even if we accept Thomas' emendations, then, there remain three such instances to account for. As Gronovius pointed out originally, Poppaea clearly testifies that she saw her husband's blood:[62] *aut quem cruorem coniugis vidi mei?* We can, therefore, safely dispense with this attempt to account for the ambiguities.

Maas also found Poppaea's narrative ambiguous, but offered yet another solution.[63] He argued that Seneca thereby deliberately made the dream correspond to either event: that is, whatever might happen, there would be something in this cryptic dream which pointed in the right direction. This compromise itself raises difficulties. Even granted that Seneca actually wrote the scene, some explanation would still be called for as to why he operated with this particular set of alternatives – and why he operated with alternatives at all. As we have seen, these alternatives are not mutually exclusive. In any event, this *vaticinium* is and remains ambiguous. Are we, then, to believe that it made no difference to Seneca whether his tragedy seemed to foreshadow the death of the tyrant Nero or of one of Poppaea's former husbands?

Thomas and Maas both recognized the presence of ambiguities and the necessity to provide an explanation which accounted for them. To that extent I am in agreement with them. Their attempts to emend the text or to adduce its "vagueness" as an argument in favour of Senecan authorship is nonetheless a further example of the tendency shown by all those involved in this discussion to treat the matter as an isolated issue. It is always the chronological impact of these few verses which is debated, never the adequacy of this approach, never the function of the ambiguities in the dream or in the *Octavia* as a whole. I find this atomistic approach inadequate.

Clearly, Poppaea's dream is more than a mere indicator of the *terminus post quem* of the play. For the principals, the meaning of the signs is a matter of life and death. What is more, the question of whose death is foreshadowed by this scene is surely vital to the plot and overall significance of the play, and ought not to be treated as if the rest of the play consisted of nothing but a collection of equally cryptic *termini post quos*. The resolution of this question must be integrated in an interpretation of the rest of the *Octavia*. This I propose to do in the second section.

... le contexte, au sens où nous l'entendons, ne se situe pas à côté des oeuvres ...; il n'est pas tant juxtaposé au texte que sous-jacent à lui. Plus encore qu'un contexte, il constitue un sous-texte qu'une lecture savante doit déchiffrer dans l'épaisseur même de l'oeuvre par un double mouvement, une démarche alternée de détour et de retour.

J.P. Vernant, *Mythe et tragédie* p. 23

II. 1. The *thalamus* and the sword

Some twenty years ago Herington wrote:

> "If one is willing to follow his (the author's) methods closely one will have to admit that he shapes his material with extraordinary cunning and with a symmetry of design that is paralleled in no other ancient play."[64]

As we shall see, this tendency is greatly in evidence in the two dream scenes of the play. Their similarity of composition and function can be viewed as an authorial technique for stressing the basic antagonism between Octavia and Poppaea. The similarities are of three types:

1. *The dramatic setting:* both empresses have awoken in fear,[65] both tell their nurses what they have dreamed – either in or in front of the imperial *thalamus*.
2. *The action of the dreams:* part of each dream is set in the empress' bed-chamber (the *thalamus*)[66] and each features an avenging fury (118ff; 721ff). In each dream there are people who exhibit fear[67] and at the end of each Nero kills somebody with his sword.[68] These four motives – the *thalamus*, the *avenging fury*, the display of *fear* and the *sword* – are, as we shall see, of crucial importance.
3. *The type of dream:* both dreams operate at two levels, psychological and oracular, thereby revealing the hopes and fears of the dreamer while mystically alluding to the future of the two empresses. Both dreams fall into the category of what I shall term frustration dreams.

This last designation merits some clarification before we turn to the interpretation of these particular dreams. A well-defined body of dreams in classical – particularly Roman – literature, features the representation of the dreamer's wishes as realities: whatever the dreamer finds unfavourable is transformed into its own opposite.[69]

Such dreams may be described as a conflict between two opposed groups of semantic features. The result of the conflict is usually the total victory of the features representing the wishes of the person dreaming. Thus, in the dreams, the worried are reassured, the thirsty drink, the starving eat, and frustrated or hopeful lovers make love.[70]

Some of these dream scenes, however, present themselves not as the result of a conflict but as the conflict itself. In these instances, the party representing the wishes of the person dreaming has not succeeded entirely in taking control. The dream becomes a battlefield of the hopes and fears of the person dreaming, a tormented shift between contrasting visions. Two things can then happen – the wish is ultimately fulfilled, or the dreamer's hopes are frustrated.

The dream of Quintus Cicero – at a time when he was anxious about the fate of his brother Marcus[71] – is an example of the former type, a dream of wish-fulfilment. Quintus dreamed that he was watching Marcus cross a river on horseback.[72] When Marcus suddenly *fell* into the river, disappearing from sight, Quintus trembled with *fear*, but in a moment Marcus *emerged*, mounted on the same horse and with *cheerful countenance* ascended the opposite bank where the two brothers embraced.

Vergil furnishes an example of the contrary type of dream – that in which the dreamer's hopes are frustrated – in his comparison of Turnus' final despair with the dreams in which one strives "to run ever onward but fails and falls down fainting at the moment of greatest effort."[73]

Commenting on this Homeric dream simile, Donatus makes the general observation that all human beings have had this kind of dream in which one wishes to do what one cannot and in which everything seems to come to nothing.[74] For our purposes it is significant to note that the literary means of conveying this type of conflict is that of semantic opposition. The juxtaposition of *teneo* and *sequor*, of *captum* and *volucrem* in this Horatian frustration dream is an instance of this semantic opposition:

"Nocturnis ego somniis
iam *captum teneo,* iam *volucrem sequor*
te per gramina Martii
campi te per aquas, dure, volubilis."[75]

Similarly, the thirsty man dreams that he drinks but still suffers from thirst,[76] the desperate man wavers between hope and despair,[77] the lonely man cannot find the one he seeks,[78] and the lost man wanders without coming upon the path.[79]

Porphyrion interpreted Horace's dream as a conflict between his hope (*ex desiderio*) and his fear (*terrore quodam mentis*).[80] Psychological interpretations on these lines appear to have been current in the imperial age.[81] They were often, however, tailored to merge with traditional religious beliefs, particularly in those genres where the profession (if no more) of such beliefs was *de rigueur*. In many of the dream scenes of Roman literature, both divine and psychological motivation were distinguished without any sense of inconsistency – the two lines of interpretation, being parallel, need not meet.[82] Hercules' dream in Valerius Flaccus is both a prophetic dream inspired by a god and a reflection of Hercules' longing for Hylas and the futility of his attempts to recover him:[83] in other words, a "frustration dream."

Both of the dreams in the *Octavia* belong to this category. They presuppose similar ideas as to how dreams work, and similar modes of describing the personal experience in ancient literature. Both dreams (as we shall see) exhibit an unequalled wealth of semantic oppositions – among them the ambiguities which have for centuries bewildered those trying to puzzle out the date and authorship of the *Octavia*. Yet the "problems" connected with these ambiguities dissolve on recognition of the code which rendered the dream scenes intelligible to a contemporary audience. It becomes apparent that the ambiguities serve the same end as the semantic oppositions in other such dreams – giving expression to the conflict between the fate feared by the dreamer and the desired goal.

Let us now approach the interpretation of the two dream scenes with this in mind. A vital element of the interpretation is the treatment of the four motives which the dreams share. These motives are: the *thalamus*, the *fury*, the *sword*, and *fear*.

The dramatic setting of the *Octavia* and the concatenation of scenes often have a symbolic significance. It is not fortuitous that the play opens in Octavia's *thalamus*, that part of the action of her dream takes place there, and that it is in (or in front of)* the *thalamus* that she tells the nurse of her dream. The *thalamus* and the *torus* are recurrent symbols in the play of the status and power of the empress.[84] The fall of Octavia and the rise of Poppaea are described in terms of two opposed movements, one leading away from the *thalamus*, and one toward it.

In the first scene Octavia is in the *thalamus* and is still Nero's wife. On her second appearance she is outside the imperial palace – she has been evicted from the *thalamus*.[85] In the final scene of the play she is already on her way to exile and death.[86]

Poppaea's course is the reverse of this. In the first scene she *imminet thalamis meis*, as Octavia expresses it.[87] As Octavia leaves the *thalamus*, it has already been occupied by Poppaea.[88] An indignant Roman populace determines to drag her from the imperial bed.[89]

"What have they done, what is their plan?" asks the chorus on hearing of the revolt (788).

The messenger replies:

"Reddere penates Claudiae divi parant
torosque fratris, debitam partem imperi." (789-90)

The populace does not, however, succeed in carrying out this aim.

Poppaea has meanwhile told her nurse her dream. It is significant that in this scene – the only one in which she actually appears – she emerges from her *thalamus in tears* (690ff). The nurse's attempts to comfort her and persuade her to re-enter the chamber are unsuccessful.[90] Poppaea is ill at ease and asks the nurse to pray for her, for the dream seems to portend that her admission to the room will ultimately prove fatal to herself and to Nero.

* Cf. the appendix p. 58ff.

It was in this ill-fated chamber that Octavia in her initial lament had recorded the fates of her mother, her father and her brother – to all of whom imperial power proved fatal. She likens herself to Electra – but an Electra whose Orestes has already died, whose hope for revenge has long since been frustrated and who lives only to lament her dead (57ff). She might thus be best described as a frustrated avenger, as she wavers between hope and despair, praying for revenge and wishing she were dead, planning to kill Nero with her own hands while accepting her impending fate as inevitable. She can hope for aid from none but the dead – and, as her nurse points out, the dead do not seem to care (137ff).

This conflict between hope and despair manifests itself in her dreams: everything she could hope for turns out here to be inseparably linked to everything she fears. Night after night she sees Britannicus' sad shade (115ff) – sadness being an unfavourable sign.[91] At first, though, her prayers seem to have been heard. The dead do seem to care: he appears before her as an *avenging fury* – a recurrent motif of the play, and one of the four which the two dreams have in common. Here the motif has taken on a strangely feeble form: bearing torches, Britannicus tries to reach Nero's eyes and face to punish him, but events take a surprising turn and he fails. The traditional roles of fury and villain are reversed and instead of fleeing, Nero drives the fury to flight, instead of being punished the criminal commits his crime twice over:

"Quam saepe tristis umbra germani meis
offertur oculis, membra cum solvit quies
et fessa fletu lumina oppressit sopor:
modo facibus atris armat infirmas manus
oculosque et ora fratris infestus petit,
modo trepidus idem refugit in thalamos meos;
persequitur hostis atque inhaerenti mihi
violentus ensem per latus nostrum rapit." (115-22)

We discern in this the tendency of the frustration dream to relate things, actions, and persons to two opposed semantic fields of which one is favourable, the other unfavourable to the dreaming person. The opposition between the two fields is underlined by anaphoric adverbs (*modo ... modo* 118-20), a stylistic feature to be found in other dream scenes of this type.[92] The protagonists both fulfil a dual and conflicting set of functions: Britannicus embodies Octavia's (frail) hopes of revenge and their subsequent frustration. Within the same scene, he is described as both weak and armed (*armat infirmas* 118), he is a frightened,[93] not frightening, and a fleeing, not persecuting fury.[94] The semantic features usually associated with avenging furies are in this description either subordinated to or replaced by semantic features usually associated with the victims of such furies. Nero's treatment is the opposite. He also fulfils a dual set of functions: at first haunted by an avenging fury, he is by the end of the dream – contrary to what might be expected – the persecuting,[95] not fleeing, the terrifying, not terrified, figure. Here it is the criminal, not the fury, who is armed, and the fury, not the criminal, who is attacked.

Then something unexpected happens. In the final lines of Octavia's dream the initial antagonism between Nero and Britannicus, which had appeared to indicate that Nero would simply repeat his murder of Britannicus, takes a new course, so that in killing Britannicus, Nero also kills Octavia – or is it only Octavia whom he kills? Her words are ambiguous. If we take *inhaerenti* as referring to Britannicus the meaning of these two lines seems to be that Britannicus is clinging to Octavia (*mihi* 121) as Nero drives his sword through – whom?

A great number of translators, among them Miller, Thomann and Watling have taken *latus nostrum* as a *sing. pro plur.: both our bodies, unser beider Leib, both our sides* – and that is surely possible. But the problem is, that if we take *inhaerenti* as referring to Octavia, the lines suggest a different meaning: that it is through *her* side (*nostrum = meum*) that Nero drives his sword.[96]

It is Ballaira who has pointed this out – without, however, giving due attention to the fact that this ambiguous conclusion is paralleled in Poppaea's dream. This passage has never been studied as closely as the former, though the translations again exhibit significant variations: usually both of them are said to die but Nuce, Greslou and Gustafsson are either ambiguous or suggest the alternative, that only Octavia dies. Helm took the rather extreme position that Octavia could not have witnessed her own death and insists that Britannicus alone is killed.[97] One of his reasons seems to have been that Octavia did not actually die by Nero's hands: that, at least, was what offended another scholar.[98] Need I repeat that these dreams do not give a detailed rendering of reality so much as portray the future in a general way by means of conventional signs? And is it not, furthermore, rather excessive to treat this scene as exceptional when there is in fact a scene quite as ambiguous in the dream recounted by another empress to another nurse later in the very same play? There are, furthermore, a number of instances in classical literature of the use of ambiguity in prophecies for dramatic effect. In dream scenes it highlights the perfidy of courtiers and the vanity of the reckless while investing the self-delusions of the doomed and the pessimism of the miserable with a tragic quality.[99]

I see no reason, therefore, to pass over the ambiguities in this dream scene as being of no particular significance. Still less when one reflects that the sudden shift in the focus of attention at the end of Octavia's dream from Britannicus to herself is dramatically consistent and completely in character. We have seen that Britannicus stands for Octavia's hopes of revenge and their frustration. His attempt to punish Nero is also hers, and likewise his failure. Since he is her *alter ego*, it is, therefore, only logical that they should share an identical fate in the dream. Their joint death is a prophecy that she will share the fate of her brother, and is, on the psychological level, a testimony that even in her dreams Octavia cannot delude herself about her desperate situation.

It is, nonetheless, highly significant that the dream admits of an alternative interpretation. The ambiguous conclusion seems to suggest that it is with *her* fate that the dream is concerned, *even when it speaks of Britannicus*. It highlights her miserable solitude, which is relieved only by her own fantasies. The avenger is a mere figment of her imagination and the symbolic re-enactment of his death is a fearful and all too obvious parable. Truly

"Me dira miseri fata germani trahunt" (182).

Let us now take a closer look at Nero's behaviour in this scene. Here, as in Poppaea's dream, Nero appears with a *sword* in his hand, and in both of the dreams there are people who show *fear*.

These are, it will be remembered, the third and fourth of the motives which the two dreams have in common. Nor is this correspondence fortuitous. Just as the *thalamus* is the recurrent symbol of the empress' status and power, so the sword is a symbol of the emperor's position in this play.

The sword was in general a common symbol of imperial power,[100] of the *ius necis vitaeque civium*,[101] but Nero's reign was in the official propaganda celebrated initially as the return of the Golden Age, a period of peace and true clemency.[102] It was, one poet claims, an age that did not know the drawn sword.[103] According to Seneca, the young Nero could justly say of himself:

"Conditum, immo constrictum apud me ferrum est, summa parsimonia etiam vilissimi sanguinis."[104]

No one, says Seneca, had been entrusted with the sword at an earlier age than Nero, and still he could boast of not having shed a single drop of blood.[105]

But things had changed since Seneca wrote *De clementia*. In the *Octavia*, Nero no longer shows the clemency which Seneca advocates, but feels that he must kill or be killed (462ff). Thus he insists on using his sword ruthlessly to protect himself,[106] to make the people obey,[107] and to rid himself of enemies and rivals. Octavia is one of them and, like her brother, she must die:

"Tollantur hostes ense suspecti mihi
invisa coniunx pereat et carum sibi
fratrem sequatur. Quidquid excelsum est cadat!" (469ff.)

In other words, he cannot sheathe his sword for *fear* of what might happen.[108] Fear is the inescapable shadow of Nero's exalted station: others must fear, that he may be safe.[109] Caesar pardoned Brutus, but paid for his *dementia* – as Nero calls it – with his life (496ff. Augustus was wiser, he killed his rivals, sheathing his sword at last (524-5) when "fear sufficed to hold his power secure",[110] and on his death a pious son made him a god (527ff). Nero is confident that

> "Nos quoque manebunt astra, si saevo prior
> ense occuparo quidquid infestum est mihi
> dignaque nostram subole fundaro domum." (530ff.)

In Octavia's dream he is depicted, accordingly, in the act of killing one of his enemies with the sword (122), and fear pervades the atmosphere of the dream.[111] Considering the symbolic significance of the *thalamus*, it is furthermore highly significant that the murder should take place there (120). To fulfil his stated programme Nero needs an heir, but as he tells Seneca he does not want Octavia to be the mother (533ff). He has, he says, found another worthy of his *thalamus*,[112] and she is already expecting his child. He therefore announces his intention of marrying Poppaea[113] over Seneca's protests. In the dream we see the fatal consequences of that marriage for the former occupant of the *thalamus*.

The wedding of Nero and Poppaea is a turning point in the *Octavia*. Until then Nero has been characterized as the omnipotent tyrant, but the four motives which stand for the power and status of the emperor and his consort are with that wedding transformed. *What had been the symbols of the imperial couple's future suddenly become the symbols of their undoing.*

The four-fold inversion of the power motives culminates in Poppaea's dream narrative, but it manifests itself also in the two scenes which take place while the ill-fated wedding of Nero and Poppaea is being celebrated. In the first of these scenes (593ff) the *fury* motif recurs – and the attempts of *this* avenging fury to make Nero pay for his crimes are clearly not going to be frustrated. With the appearance of the ghost of Nero's mother the dramatically effective illusion that Nero need have no fears dissolves: she predicts the fall of the tyrant and the punishments prepared for him (619ff). As ghost scenes of this type usually occur at the beginning of a play,[114] the *Octavia* might here be said to begin anew. Agrippina's appearance inaugurates a course of events which will lead ultimately to Nero's fall and death.

At this point it will be necessary to make a short digression:

As is well known, those who favour the authenticity of the play have argued that Agrippina's prophecies betray no knowledge of Nero's actual manner of death. Nobody, so runs the argument, who knew how Nero really died could have written a *vaticinium ex eventu* so vague and inaccurate.[115] As will appear, those who advocate this position have taken it for granted that prophecies of this type depict what is actually going to happen. Those who doubt the authenticity of the play have accordingly (to a certain extent) founded their case on what they regarded as realistic details in this prophecy. Nobody, so they concluded, but a person who knew how Nero really died could have written a *vaticinium ex eventu* of such accuracy.[116] – This is another example of the realistic fallacy. Thus most of the "realistic" details of Agrippina's prophecy belong to the conventional imagery employed in ancient imprecations. The fury preparing the death of the criminal and Tantalus, Ixion and Sisyphos – it is all there.[117] Even that part of the prophecy which seems to allude to Nero's actual manner of death has its precedents.[118] We cannot, therefore, deduce simply from Agrippina's words that the author of this play knew Nero died just as Suetonius has described. Equally, though, we cannot – as many scholars have done[119] – conclude that Seneca therefore wrote the play. That the man who wrote this scene uses conventional imagery indicates first and foremost that he is a Roman poet who observes the rules and conventions common to the poetry of his day. Within this mythological framework the scene does, it is true, seem to make a number of allusions to events posterior to Seneca's death, such as the Parthian embassy of 66, though some have argued otherwise.[120] This issue need not detain us further, since as I have shown it is important for my purposes only to make the point that the realistic detail of the descriptions of the characters' fates is not intended to be taken literally, but to be construed by means of conventional signs which point in a general direction of doom.

In a sense, the whole of the *Octavia* is constructed in such a way as to stress the importance of the *thalamus* – both the chamber itself and the imperial elevation which it signifies.[121] The action of the play is distributed over three days. Of these, the first and third days open with scenes in or outside the *thalamus* of the empress. The pivotal second day is dedicated to the *incoronazione* of Poppaea and the dethronement of Octavia. The wedding itself is celebrated off-stage – what the audience experiences is a wedding which has been transformed by the appearance of Agrippina's ghost into a funeral. In antiquity the contrast between and similarity of these two *rites de passage* was proverbial: in descriptions of ill-fated weddings it is often a fury who performs the offices of the *pronuba*,[122] it is music fit for a funeral rather than for a wedding which one hears,[123] and the *thalamus* is likened to a tomb, the *torus* to a hearse.[124] The ill-omened weddings of the imperial family are all described in this manner in the *Octavia*: thus, a fury attended Messalina's second marriage and quenched the fire of the nuptial torches in blood; her immorality brought about her own death and that of her husband and son (262ff). At Claudius' subsequent marriage to his niece – an incestuous union which was to cause crime and murder – a torch-bearing fury entered the palace, *sancta Pietas* fled – Claudius was poisoned (141ff). Yet another torch-bearing fury – embodied in this case in Agrippina – attended the ill-fated wedding of Nero and Octavia:

"Illa, illa meis tristis Erinys
thalamis Stygios praetulit ignes."(23-4)

The fury motif is thus used in such a way that it creates a metonymic relation[125] between these weddings and their fatal consequences: present is thereby described as future, cause as effect, weddings as if they were already funerals.

This tendency culminates in the celebration of the wedding of Nero and Poppaea: there, in the ghost scene, the *fury-pronuba* actually appears on stage, a Stygian torch in her hand, to celebrate the funeral-wedding:

"Tellure rupta Tartaro gressum extuli,
Stygiam cruenta praeferens dextra facem
thalamis scelestis: nubat his flammis meo
Poppaea nato iuncta, quas vindex manus
dolorque matris vertet ad tristes rogos." (593ff)

The subsequent scenes emphasize the funereal and sinister aspects of Nero's and Poppaea's wedding. While it is being celebrated in the palace the populace plans to tear down Poppaea's statues and to drag Poppaea herself from the imperial *torus* (686ff).

The third day opens in a way which reminds us ominously of the fate of the former occupant of the *thalamus*[126]: again an empress recounts to her nurse a terrifying dream. The reaction of the bewildered nurse underlines the sinister contrast between the triumph and jubilation of the wedding and the things Poppaea dreamed. According to the nurse, the wedding day had been the answer to all their hopes and prayers.[127] It had been *celebrated* as magnificently as that of Peleus and Thetis,[128] but in the dream these hopes are, as we know, all frustrated. There one finds a much less reassuring analogy:

"...Visa nam thalamos meos
celebrare turba est maesta..." – and
not a happy crowd.[129]

The concatenation of wedding and funeral imagery is a pattern which repeats itself throughout the former half of the dream narrative. The dream is not, however, a mere repetition of the ghost scene – it transcends it.[130] In the dream, the *fury-pronuba* grimly takes her task to its logical conclusion and installs Poppaea in what turns out to be an infernal *thalamus*.[131] It is no longer one of Nero's enemies, but his empress, Poppaea, who feels *fear*.

The author has taken pains to show how everything Poppaea had hoped for was annihilated in the mirror of her fears: instead of merriment, the women of Rome expressed their sorrow at her wedding;[132] instead of invoking Hymen, they lamented her fate;[133] instead of the marriage *tibiae* she heard the funeral *tubae*,[134] and instead of the marriage torch it was the blood-stained torch of an avenging fury which her fierce and menacing *pronuba*, Agrippina, waved before her (722ff). Agrippina had been murdered by Nero to gratify Poppaea (125ff), and it is only just that she should be the agent of retribution on this occasion. Her appearance is also well motivated from a psychological viewpoint: avenging furies could symbolize the torments and fears of a guilty conscience to the Roman mind.[135]

Poppaea's *deductio* is indeed a striking expression of her fears: she was dragged along, terror-stricken, by the *fury-pronuba*,[136] the earth opened before her feet and she fell, head foremost (725ff) – whereas Roman brides were usually lifted across the threshold to ensure they did not stumble.[137] The *fury-pronuba* led the moribund bride to her infernal bridal suite[138] where a weary Poppaea sat down on the *torus*.[139]

At this point in the ritual a Roman groom would normally be expected to enter the *thalamus*.[140] In the distorting mirror of Poppaea's fears, this part of the wedding ceremony is transformed into a scene, rich in striking contrasts, which culminates in armed conflict between Poppaea's former and present husbands – and all they stand for. It is Poppaea's previous husband and not the groom who first enters her *thalamus*.[141] His entry effectively underlines the contrast between Poppaea's past and present. He is accompanied by their child and a throng of friends. The *comitante turba*,[142] the child and the signs of affection and love – all of which a Roman matron might well hope to see in a dream on her wedding night. The problem, though, is that it is a recollection of bygone happiness, not a prophecy of future glory which Poppaea sees while lying in Nero's arms. Thus the overall tendency of these dreams to take back with one hand what has been granted by the other manifests itself in this scene also: her hopes for a happy marriage express themselves in her dream, but are seemingly cancelled out by their firm relegation to the past.

The groom's arrival bears an even stronger stamp of frustration. There is no trace of the festivity and jubilation of the actual wedding in his entry.[143] As in Octavia's dream, he is here entering his wife's *thalamus* with a sword in his hand.[144] Here, though, as we have seen, it is no longer his enemies who are in fear. In Octavia's dream, Britannicus was terrified, but now it is Nero.[145] The fear which Nero then inspired seems here to recoil upon its author and the sword with which he murders Crispinus seems also to be turned against himself. The motives which connote his power have in other words been inverted: now they also foreshadow his fall. The dream thus visualizes Nero's tyrannic, brutal reign *and* its consequences for himself – just as it visualizes Poppaea's criminal wedding and its consequences for her. It links the fate of the cruel tyrant with that of his victim. It is, in short, a prophecy that Nero will share the fate of Crispinus.

The gradual inversion of the power motives in this scene and in the scenes preceding it *has* prepared us for this culmination. If it had not been for the problem of authenticity, this ultimate ambiguity would long since have been recognized as the logical outcome of it all. The ambiguity of Poppaea's questions and the interpretation alike serve to force upon us the moral that he who lives by the sword shall die by the sword.

Poppaea's final words are a request for her nurse to pray for her:

"Tu vota pro me suscipe et precibus piis
superos adora, maneat ut praesens status."[146]

We know the prayers will be in vain: her very *status* will be her undoing.

There is much that is arresting in the manner in which these two dreams have been contrasted. Their repetition of the four power motives, the two chiastically opposed inversions and the employment, twice over, of the traditional frustration dream scheme for this operation – such a pair of dreams is, indeed, a unique phenomenon in ancient drama.[147] In my book on Vergil, I examined his technique of using a uniform pair of dreams to lay bare the contrast between Aeneas and Turnus from their first appearance in the plot. In the *Pharsalia*, Lucan employed a similar device to highlight the contrast between Caesar and Pompey.[148] It is, I think, against this background that our pair of dreams should be seen. Here, too, the symmetry of design serves to emphasize the antagonism between two protagonists and their diverse fates: one figures an Electra embracing her brother to protect him from their enemy, the other a Clytemnestra embracing her former husband in her bizarre and crowded *thalamus* – a symbol of chastity opposed to one of depravity.

The ambiguous manner in which their fates are foreshadowed has its precedents in ancient drama: the fearful dilemma which faces Poppaea has justly been compared with that of Clytemnestra in Sophocles' *Electra*.[149] It should, however, be kept in mind that in

Poppaea's and Octavia's case, the alternatives are not mutually exclusive; nor does the fulfilment of their dreams take place within the play. As with some of the prophecies in Roman epic poetry and, we may safely assume, in the republican *praetextae*,[150] they serve to suggest, not a dramatic *dénouement*, but a grand historical perspective. It is within that perspective that Nero's divorce from Octavia in A.D. 62 stands revealed as a turning point in his reign – and in the history of Rome.

The "pro-Senecans" would have us believe that this perspective is the fabric of Seneca's wishful thinking. I shall not repeat all the objections to this idea – or, indeed, to the idea that Seneca wrote this play – but confine myself to three of them:

1. In Poppaea's dream, Crispinus, Nero and Poppaea herself appear in the order in which their deaths actually occurred. The comparison with similar dream scenes corroborates Chickering's hypothesis, that this may somehow be significant: in a number of instances, the order in which things are narrated corresponds to what happened.[151]

2. In both of the dreams in this play Nero is presented as murderer, first of Octavia, then of Crispinus. Need I reiterate that the objection from accuracy is invalid? The author's concern is to show Nero's involvement – and indeed he was: both died upon his bidding.

3. There is, finally, the circumstance that this murderous act in Poppaea's frustration dream has taken on a form which seems also to forebode Nero's miserable suicide; and the reference to his throat. We cannot, as we have seen, *expect* anything like accuracy in prophecies of this sort: in Agrippina's ghost scene, for instance, there is another reference to Nero's throat being cut, but there the details differ (629ff). But can we overlook the possibility of topical allusion? Such allusions would stress the *fides*[152] of the prophecy – and in this particular case it suits the author's purpose admirably.

In other words: the arguments in favour of taking Nero's death in June 68 A.D. as the *terminus post quem* of the *Octavia* are overwhelming, but if the *Octavia* was not written by Seneca it is still, in a sense, Seneca's tragedy:[153] it is imbued with his thought and it deplores his tragic failure to appease and restrain the tyrant.

Thus, when contemplating the murder-suicide scene, which we have here discussed, who of his admirers would not be reminded of Seneca's "prophetic" warnings to Nero in the *De clementia?*

> "..cum invisus sit (sc. tyrannus) quia timetur, timeri vult, quia invisus est, et illo exsecrabili versu, qui multos dedit praecipites, utitur:
> *Oderint dum metuant!*
> (...)
> Talem virum a tergo sequitur eversio, odia, venena, gladii."[154]

II. 2. "Victoria populi Romani"

Any prophecy of defeat is also a prophecy of victory. But whose, in this case? Nero's fall and the concomitant collapse of the world is presaged in terms so metaphysical as to give few precise indicators of the means of his death and the identity of his successor, leaving us with little from which to date this celebration of his fall. Seneca's monologue on the decay and imminent cataclysm associates Nero's reign with a universal degeneracy, and shows the usual millennial picture of the collapse which the wicked world brings down upon itself partly by its own momentum and partly by divine agency:

> "Collecta vitia per tot aetates diu
> in nos redundant: saeculo premimur gravi,
> quo *scelera* regnant, saevit *impietas* furens
> *turpi libido Venere* dominatur potens,
> *luxuria* victrix orbis immensas opes
> iam pridem avaris manibus, ut perdat, rapit." (430ff)

Such apocalyptic vagueness leaves us without the means to reconstruct the historical setting of the work.

Perhaps we should look elsewhere for the clues. It has generally escaped notice that Nero is fast relinquishing not only his divine mandate, but his mandate from the *people*. Of the two choruses[155] in the *Octavia*, one favours Poppaea, the other Octavia. It is instructive to examine the attitudes expressed by this second chorus, which, in a sense, is the voice of the people of Rome. At its first appearance, it behaves as choruses customarily do in ancient drama: its members raise and comment on such topics as the rumour of divorce. The notable feature of this discussion is the allusion to the *libido* of tyrants and the fates of Lucretia and Verginia.[156] In these republican legends, *libido*[157] symbolized a threat against the liberty of the people of Rome. The chorus – and thus the author – likens Octavia to Lucretia and Verginia and Nero's crimes against her to those of Tarquinius and Appius Claudius:

> "Vera priorum virtus quondam
> Romana fuit verumque genus
> Martis in illis sanguisque viris.
> Illi reges hac expulerunt
> urbe superbos ultique tuos
> sunt bene manes..." (291ff)

The equation of the republican legends and the events of A.D. 62 seems to hold a foreboding – of open conflict between a lustful tyrant and a people avenging an innocent Lucretia. At the second appearance of the chorus, the dim foreboding has become a reality.

In the palace, meanwhile, Seneca comes out on the side of the people, repeatedly warning Nero of their reaction. Nero, however, is fearful and suspicious of those who enjoy the *favor populi*. He is prepared to take the risk and, if necessary, force his will upon them:

SEN "Vix sustinere possit hos thalamos dolor
     videre populi, sancta nec pietas sinat.
NER Prohibebor unus facere quod cunctis licet?
SEN Maiora populus semper a summo exigit.
NER Libet experiri, viribus fractus meis
     an cedat animis temere conceptus favor." (572ff; cf. 455ff.)

Which is precisely what he will have to do. As Seneca had predicted, the people will not tolerate the divorce. At the sight of Octavia leaving the palace the chorus once again invokes its republican ancestors:

> "Ubi Romani vis est populi,
> fregit claros quae saepe duces,
> dedit invictae leges patriae,
> fasces dignis civibus olim,
> iussit bellum pacemque, feras
> gentes domuit, captos reges
> carcere clausit? Gravis, en, oculis

> undique nostris iam Poppaeae
> fulget imago, iuncta Neroni." (676ff)

This time their actions suit their words. They raise their call for the overthrow of statues – the traditional prelude to popular revolts in ancient Rome.[158]

The revolt is clearly not directed against the Principate as such. Rather, in defending Octavia's dynastic rights, the people clearly aims to preserve the established order (cf. 789ff and 891ff). The revolt is nonetheless an attempt of the once sovereign *populus* to prove itself worthy of its republican ancestors. The vindication of their just demand – Octavia's reinstatement – would also be the vindication of their right to have a say in such matters.[159]

The characterization of the revolt is in sharp contrast to Tacitus' account. In his detestation of mobs, he plays down the heroism of their attempt to defend Octavia and represents the revolt as a confused and ill-conceived affair.[160]

Although most of the sources agree in charging Nero with starting the fire of Rome,[161] this author stands alone in his assertion that the princeps' purpose was to harm the people.[162] We see a Nero insane with fury and hatred, wishing to subdue the people with fire, famine and want so that they will never again be able to rebel against him:

> "Malis domanda est et gravi semper iugo
> premenda ne quid simile temptare audeat
> ....
> ......Fracta per poenas metu
> parere discet principis nutu sui." (839ff)

The final scene is therefore imbued with defeat – that of the people, as of Octavia. For the third time, the chorus harks back to republican Rome, comparing her fate with that of the Gracchi and Livius Drusus, heroic champions of the popular cause. Like her they enjoyed the *favor populi,* but were defeated (882ff).

For an imperial author, this presentation of the popular stance is strikingly positive.[163] There is no hint of the usual *'panem et circenses*' image. The playwright here charts sympathetically the change in the people's attitude to Nero during the crisis of A.D. 62. Without being opposed to the principate, they gradually become alienated from their princeps, while Nero, contemptuous and hostile from the start, is transformed by the revolt into their deadly enemy. If it had not been for the allusions to the Lucretia/Verginia legends and the prophecies of Nero's imminent fall, the people's prospects would appear to be desperate. As it is, we know that all this will change with his death.

There is to my knowledge only one body of evidence from this period which exhibits a comparable sympathy and even preoccupation with the "people of Rome" and its weal – the coinage of Galba and of Vespasian. This coinage has attracted the interest of numismatists and historians because of the insight it offers in the politics and propaganda of the turbulent period after Nero's fall, but it does not seem to have been adduced in support of any of the various attempts to determine the date of the play. The arguments in favour of a date in the first century,[164] before the publication of Quintilian's *Institutiones*[165] and after the death of Nero, in the first years of the Flavians[166] – to name but the most likely – are based on other sorts of evidence.

In so far as the coinage reflects the propaganda of the rebels and the emperors Galba, Otho, Vitellius and Vespasian none of them can be said to have advertised his concern for "Mankind", for the "Senate and People of Rome" and, above all, for the "People of Rome" as strongly and variated as did Galba. To judge from Sydenham and Mattingly's *Roman Imperial Coinage* more than half of the legends and slogans with which the coinage of this period identified a specific cause with that of the P(opulus) R(omanus)* appear on the so-called anonymous coins which Galba and his followers[167] issued in the short period between his proclaiming himself *legatus Senatus ac populi Romani*[168] (April 68) and Nero's suicide in June 68 A.D. In this period the rebels countermarked Nero's coins with the legends P.R and S.P.Q.R[169] and in their own coinage references to the S.P.Q.R and, more commonly, the P.R

---

* See the table with legends from their coinage p. 44-45.

tend to replace[170] such legends as AUGUSTI – or they appear where formerly there had been none. One instance is the coins with the legend SIGNA P.R – Nero's similar type had been uninscribed;[171] another is the legend VESTA P.R. QUIRITIUM – on Nero's coins she had simply been VESTA.[172] The meaning is clear: here, with us, and not with Nero, are VESTA and the standards of the Roman people! Similarly, where the Neronian coinage exhibited legends like GENIO AUGUSTI, SECURITAS AUGUSTI, and VICTORIA AUGUSTI the rebels advertised their dedication to the GENIO P.R.[173] and promised SECURITAS P.R.[174] and the VICTORIA P.R.

In the war of propaganda let loose by the uprisings in Spain and Gaul the coins were of course only a medium of minor importance. Rumours, ballads, letters and proclamations were the channels through which the slogans of the rebels, in oral or written form, spread most rapidly. We hear of anti-Neronian ballads in Spain even before Galba had proclaimed himself; details of Vindex' abusive edicts reached Nero at Naples and he had to ask the Senate take counter measures; Galba advertised his programme in edicts to the provinces and called on all to aid the common cause.[175] By far the greatest part of this propaganda is irrevocably lost but there is every reason to believe that the coins of the period do reflect the general tenor of the rebels' slogans and catchwords. It is wellknown, for instance, that one of their war-cries was the demand for revenge – which, because of the instigators name, apparently captured the imagination of the public: in the last days of Nero opposition is said to have manifested itself in the apparently innocuous cries for *Vindicem* heard throughout the capital.[176] Vindex, in a letter, called on Galba as the *assertor* of mankind; the slogan conformed admirably with the declared intentions of the rebels: the *assertor* was a *vindex alienae libertatis*. Later Vespasian claimed the title for himself – and Pliny used it of Vindex.[177] But the slogan is already present in the coinage of the early revolt where one finds figures and legends like IUPPITER LIBERATOR, HERCULES ADSERTOR, MARS ADSERTOR, MARS ULTOR, MARTI ULTORI, and VOLKANUS ULTOR;[178] on some of them we are told more clearly what revenge will bring:[179] a representation of Mars is accompanied by the legend ADSER-

TOR LIBERTATIS and one of Nemesis by the legend SALUS GENERIS HUMANI.[180]

Galba's exploitation of the symbols of liberty and manumission (*pilleus* and *vindicta*) for political purposes is yet another example of the way the coins reflect contemporary propaganda. He made his first proclamation against Nero on a day set for the granting of freedom to slaves, he exhorted Verginius Rufus in letters to join with him for the preservation of the empire and the liberty of the Romans, and when the Roman people at the death of Nero finally was set free they ran into the streets of Rome wearing the cap of liberty.[181] From the very outset of the revolt these symbols also appear on the coins: they display the cap of liberty on the head of a *togatus*, between the daggers of Brutus and, on Galba's coins, as the attribute of *Libertas*.[182] On the latter coins *Libertas* also holds the *vindicta*. the *pilleus* and *vindicta*, the slogans *adsertor* and *vindex*, and the ceremonial at Galba's first proclamation against Nero – in all of it a grand legal metaphor is at work: That of a *causa liberalis* securing universal manumission.[183]

To summarize: such evidence as we have to hand suggests that the coinage does reflect the general tenor of Galba's anti-Neronian propaganda and that this propaganda was, to a great extent, of a populist kind directed at convincing the populace that Galba, not Nero, was the true friend of the Roman people.[184] To the legends from the early coinage quoted above I add the, at times, very striking legends in the coinage of Galba which suggest that his aims were identical with theirs: thus he celebrated Nero's fall as the VICTORIA P.R, he advertised LIBERTAS P.R and SECURITAS P.R; in one instance *Victoria* is displayed inscribing P.R on a shield and Galba was even styled AUGUSTUS P.R – the people's emperor![185]

A comparison with the coins of Otho, Vitellius and Vespasian which exhibit the legend P.R throws into relief the populism of Galba's coinage:

LEGEND	DATE	RIC. VOL, PAGE, NUMBER and KIND
Anonymous coins:[186]		
FLORENTE FORTUNA P.R	68	I 184 1 D
GENIUS P.R[187]	68	I 184 3 D; 10 Au
		185 11;14 D
		187 32 D
		191 10 D
GENIO P.R	68	I 181.1-4;6 D
		182 14 D
		184 2 D
GEN P.R[188]	68	I 185[1] D
G.P.R	68	I 184 9 Au
LIBERTAS P.R. RESTITUTA	68	I 182 9;10 D
PAX P.R	68	I 182 16 D
		190 4 Au
PACI P.R	68	I 182 11-13 D
SECURITAS P.R	68	I 187 30 Au; 31,32 D
SIGNA P.R	68	I 187 33 Au; 34-39 D
VESTA P.R. QUIRITIUM[189]	68	I 190 4 D
		191 6;7;9;11 D
VICTORIA P.R	68	I 183 27 D
		189 23 D
Galba:		
AUGUSTUS P.R	68-9	I 207 77 D
LIBERTAS P.R	68-9	I 200 11 D
SECURITAS P. ROMANI S.C[190]	68-9	I 217 168 As
VICTORIA P.R	68-9	I 201 23 Au
		212 126 Au; 127 D
VICTORIA P.R.S.C	68-9	I 213 134 D
VICTORIA[191]	68-9	I 212 128 D
(*Victoria* inscribing P.R on a shield)		
Otho:		
SECURITAS P.R	69	I 219 11 Au; 12 D

LEGEND		RIC. VOL, PAGE, DATE NUMBER and KIND		
Vitellius:				
CONCORDIA P.R	69	I	224	1 Au; 2 D
SECURITAS P. ROMANI S.C[192]	69	I	222	
VESTA P.R. QUIRITIUM	69	I	231	7 Au; 8 D
Vespasian:				
AETERNITAS P.R.S.C	69-70	II	61 384	As
	70		65 408	S
GENIUM P.R	69-70	II	51 307	D
SECURITAS P. ROMANI S.C	70	II	66 412a	As
	71		72 479	Dp
SECURITAS P.R[193]	69-71	II	17 22a	Au
PAX P. ROMANI S.C[194]	71	II	69 440	S
Titus[195] { CONGIAR PRIMUM P.R. DAT S.C	72	II	86 606	S
GENI. P.R.S.C	76	II	94 677	As

The table indicates a drastic fall in the references to the P.R in the coinage of Otho and Vitellius: discarding the variations of inflexion and abbreviation, there are 8 different slogans in the coinage of the early revolt and 5 more in Galba's, but only 3 – or 4 – in that of Otho and Vitellius. The latter two were both adversaries of Galba and posed as successors of Nero.[196] It is, therefore, not surprising that their coinage, as against that of Galba, is markedly less populist and exhibits a return to a more unambiguously autocratic style. Thus there is a far greater stress on the people's active support (SIGNA P.R; AUGUSTUS P.R and VICTORIA P.R) in the coinage of the early revolt and of Galba than in that of Otho and Vitellius. It is also significant that in the coinage of Galba legends like VICTORIA GALBAE AUG. and VICTORIAE IMP. GALBAE AUG. alternate with legends like VICTORIA P.R and VICTORIA IMPERI ROMANI[197] whereas Otho has only VICTORIA OTHONIS[198] and Vitellius only legends such as VICTORIA AUGUSTI, and VICTORIA IMP. GERMANICI.[199]

It is illuminating to compare the distribution of P.R legends with the LIBERTAS legends from this period: the trend is uniform. "The prominence of *Libertas* (*sc.* in Galba's coinage) is not surprising, for the various movements which brought Galba to power all proclaimed as their objects the overthrow of Nero's tyranny and the restoration of liberty."[200] But whereas Galba's coinage has legends like LIBERTAS AUGUSTA S.C *and* LIBERTAS P.R (and PUBLICA; RESTITUTA; AUG(US); AUG(UST) R.XL) there is no trace of LIBERTAS in Otho's western coinage and only two legends (e.g. LIBERTAS RESTITUTA and AUGUSTI S.C) survive on that of Vitellius.[201]

But in the first years of Vespasian's reign there was, as Kraay has put it, a "revival (or virtually continuation) of Galba's principal theme, *Libertas* ... Moreover, the Flavian type recording the offering of a wreath to the ADSERTOR LIBERTATIS PUBLICAE proves that the theme of *Libertas* was ... a concept actively favoured by the new dynasty."[202]

When things had been stabilized, however, untimely celebrations of the *people's* exploits were no longer on the agenda. Like the LIBERTAS legends,[203] those referring to the P.R seem to have fallen out of favour early in Vespasian's reign: there are three legends from 69-70 A.D; one of the two following instances quoted is dubious and with the commemoration of the *congiarium* of Titus the circle closes and the role of the POPULUS ROMANUS on the coins of its emperors is once again the old one: passive, humble, and inglorious it receives its dole ...

The picture of the revolt against Nero in A.D. 62 which we find in the *Octavia* differs on the one hand so strongly from the politics and propaganda of Otho and Vitellius while on the other corresponding so closely to the propaganda of Galba and Vespasian that there seems to be a strong case in favour of arguing that the play was written under the influence, and perhaps as part, of the propaganda of the two latter emperors.

We shall leave aside what cannot be said to be typical of that revolutionary period[204] and concentrate on three aspects of the play which would be highly unusual under normal circumstances – but not, apparently, in the short period after the fall of Nero:

1. The idealization of the *populus Romanus* and the emphasis on Nero's hatred of it.
2. The idealization of republican revolts and revolutionaries.
3. The millennial hopes for Rome's rebirth.

1. The emphasis on Nero's crimes against the people in this play is striking: the author demonstrates that Nero was never truly *popularis* and even suggests a parallel with Tarquinius Superbus and Appius Claudius; he argues that he violated their rights and deprived them of their liberty and that he finally burned off their city with the explicit purpose of doing them harm. This picture conforms almost too well with the propaganda which, in various ways, presented Galba and Vespasian as the champions of the people and the restorers of liberty and which celebrated the fall of Nero as the liberation and victory of the people.[205] Their revolt against Nero in A.D. 62 was a forerunner of the later universal revolt – that seems to be the argument of the play.

The importance attached to the people of Rome in this play may indeed seem disproportionate – but it is less so when seen in what I suggest was its proper context. On the eve of Nero's fall social discontent seems to have been widespread, but propaganda is never much given to the "who" and "why" questions so dear to the historian's heart: it concentrates rather on convincing "us" of the identity of "our" interests – and the outmoded formulae POPULUS ROMANUS and S.P.Q.R were admirable for such purposes.[206]

2. Considering the populist trend in the propaganda of this period, it is not surprising that, in some cases, it reintroduces suitable legends and symbols from the coinage of republican Rome: in theory, at least, that was the hey-day of the POPULUS ROMANUS. In fact, the people figured far less prominently in the coinage of that period than in the coinage of A.D. 68-9, but the rebels took virtually everything they could get. In a society tending to seek its Utopias in the past those symbols and legends had the enormous advantage of being traditional.

The bearded GENIUS POPULI ROMANI first figured on a republican coin issued in 76-5 B.C.[207] – and then it suddenly reappears in the anonymous coinage of 68 A.D. It is doubtful whether the republican coin did indicate *popularis* sympathies[208] –

I doubt that the rebels in 68 A.D. cared whether it did. The reintroduction of this and similar symbols and legends (like FOR-T(una) P.R. and F.P.R.)[209] helped to give their coinage the desired populist, republican, anti-Neronian, and – traditional tinge, but it is not, for all we know, based upon a wish to abolish the principate. Their aim was reform, not revolution.[210] Hence the paradox that the coinage of the emperors Galba, Vitellius and Vespasian exhibit *Libertas* with *pilleus* – a symbol which, in different designs, had been employed by *populares* in the era of the Gracchi and later;[211] hence the invocation of LIBERTAS on the coinage of those emperors – a legend which had been prominent on the coins of Brutus and Cassius;[212] hence, finally, the reappearance, in the anonymous coinage, of a *Libertas* similar to the figure adorning the coins of Cassius and, most striking of all, of the renowned Brutus coin with the *pilleus* and two daggers.[213]

We find an equally curious combination of revolutionary ideals and reformist aims in the *Octavia*. The enthusiasm for subversives such as the Gracchi and Livius Drusus is singular[214] – as is the analogy between these rebels and the empress of Rome. The comparison between the people's attempts to vindicate Octavia's as well as their own rights and the bravery of their ancestors in 510 and 449 BC. are no less striking. Romans would inevitably associate the first of these events with the establishment of the republic and with Brutus, *liberator ille populi Romani;* the second event was the classic paradigm of the *causa liberalis*, and the *adsertor* and *vindex libertatis* motives are very prominent in Livy's famous treatment of the story.[215] Again I can think of only one period where reformist aims would be formulated within that particular republican conceptual framework: it is in the short reign of Galba and the first years of the Flavians.

3. The coinage of A.D. 68-9 seems to indicate that there was an element of millenarianism in the fears and hopes which swept the Roman Empire at the end of nearly 100 years of Iulio-Claudian rule. Coached in the powerful and familar language of traditional religion, the coins present the rebels as *avengers* working in accordance not only with mankind and the people of Rome but also with the gods. They bring redemption from the tyrant, they bring SALUS GENERIS HUMANI.[216] The coins of Galba and Vespa-

sian advertised the rebirth and resurgence of Rome and Vespasian's coin with the legend AETERNITAS P.R and Victory presenting the Palladium to Vespasian suggests the advent of eternal dawn for the people of Rome.[217]

The *Octavia* is also invested with an aura of cosmic drama. There are signs in heaven and earth of Nero's imminent fall: a comet and the apocalyptic breakdown of kinship rules show that the end is at hand;[218] furies and a dream promise revenge and divine retribution. Chaos will, however, be succeeded by a return to the Golden Age; in almost ecstatic words Seneca, in his great soliloquy, beholds the cosmic cataclysm:

> "...Nunc ades mundo, dies
> supremus ille, qui premas genus impium
> caeli ruina, rursus ut stirpem novam
> generet *renascens* melior, ut quondam tulit
> iuvenis, tenente regna Saturno poli."[219]

The idea of palingenesis is of course predictable in such a context, but the choice of the expression *renascens* suggests that this is more than a "topos": the slogan

> ROMA RENASC
> ROMA RENASCES
> ROMA RENASCENS[220]

was prominent in the coinage of the early revolt as well as in that of Galba. The author of the *Octavia* had a keen eye for official propaganda and in a number of instances he has verbal quotations from the slogans of Claudius and Nero.[221] He may therefore here be quoting one of Galba's.

To summarize: as far as the evidence goes there is in my view a strong case for a date either in the reign of Galba or in the first years of Vespasian. There are strong arguments for either candidate and as Vespasian stressed the similarity of his and Galba's cause,[222] it is perhaps presumptuous to choose between the two. I think, however, that a number of circumstances make Galba's short reign (June 68 – 15th of January 69) the likelier date of the two:

1. The play leaves us in no doubt as to the imminent fall of Nero – beyond that lies a vague and dreamlike Golden Age. I doubt if anyone writing in the first years of the Flavians would have described the reign of Galba and the year of the four emperors in that way. The author *could* have sacrificed references to Otho* and Vitellius on the altar of dramatic unity but should we not, at least, expect an oracular allusion to the "avengers from East"?[223] If, on the other hand, we assume that the play was written in the reign of Galba there is nothing odd in its preoccupation with Nero and the confidence that once he had been removed things would automatically be better: "after an evil reign the fairest dawn is the first."[224]

2. The propaganda of the early revolt and of Galba seems to have left a clear stamp on the *Octavia* but if we discard the slogans adopted from the Galbans the same cannot be said of the Flavian propaganda.

3. It is noteworthy, furthermore, that the republicanism and the active role of the people in the *Octavia* conforms somewhat better with the propaganda of the former party than with that of the latter.

> "Si immensum imperii corpus stare ac librari sine rectore posset dignus eram a quo res publica inciperet: nunc eo necessitatis iam pridem ventum est ut nec mea senectus conferre plus populo Romano possit quam bonum successorem, nec tua plus iuventa quam bonum principem."

Thus Galba in Tacitus.[225] Vespasian is never, to my knowledge, described as that enthusiastic – or sentimental – about the republic.

4. At the risk of forcing the material it can be argued, finally, that the author shows a concern for the fate of the exiled nobility which conforms rather well with the restorative policy of Galba who, to a certain degree, made the cause of the exiles his own.[226]

---

* Cf. the appendix on Otho in the *Octavia* p. 61.

Granted that the political propaganda of the period did make an impact on the play this raises the question: what was its purpose? There will, inevitably, be a hypothetical element in my answer to this question: we know very little about the *fabulae praetextae* and the theatre of this period.

The republican *praetextae* had dealt with the *res gestae Romanorum*[227] and the people of Rome will have played their part. The element of patriotism and political propaganda was apparently great.[228] The Roman nobility expected immortality from poetry and they would not be disappointed in their poets. The celebrations of Roman victory at Clastidium, Ambracia and Pydna were probably written at the request of the victorious generals or their kin; the heroism of an ancestor or an admired legendary figure could also be dealt with in the *praetextae*.[229]

The advent of monarchy saw a change in the theatrical repertory. A means of keeping the populace acquiesced it could, at times, be a menace. The restrictions imposed on audiences, the necessity of the presence of soldiery at performances, and the stories of *theatralis licentia*, of discontented mobs rioting or eagerly grasping at allusions and understatements[230] – all of this goes far to explain why an eminently political genre like the *praetexta* seems to have fallen from favour. In the early reign of Vespasian, when Senatorial opposition was outspoken and tolerated, we nonetheless hear of the *praetextae* (and tragedies) of Curiatus Maternus.[231] He had, in a previous play, succesfully launched an attack on one of Nero's creatures, Vatinius. The title (*Nero?*) and the genre (a *praetexta?*) of the play is disputed – its purpose was, like some of Maternus' other plays, clearly political.[232] His plays had been recited in auditoria and in the theatres[233] and one of them (*Cato*) had strongly offended those in power.

It is difficult to form an opinion of the extent to which the author of the *Octavia* was influenced by his predecessors. It has been argued that frequent changes of scene and lack of temporal unity were not alien to the genre.[234] We know that the dream scene was not.[235] The element of republicanism with which one would be likely to associate the genre would not be unwelcome and the patently propagandistic purpose of the republican *praetextae* conformed excellently with his own. Some of the republican specimens were written to immortalize the triumph of the Roman army and its generals; the celebrations of the victories of Augustus included a performance of Varius' *Thyestes*.[236] Is it too much to suggest that the *Octavia* was written to celebrate the victory of Galba, the champion and emperor of the people of Rome? Extolling their brave and heroic stand it is effectively exposing the fallen tyrant as their enemy and, so it seems, indirectly paying homage to the emperor whose coins told them that his victory was theirs. This assumption seems to me to be the one most in accordance with the evidence we have.

Epilogue

The *Octavia* is, in a sense, a *damnatio memoriae* and in our concluding remarks we shall examine more closely what I consider to be the Galban stamp on Nero's portrait in the play.

There were various anti-Neronian manifestations during the reign of Galba. After the fall of Nero the populace paraded the *pilleus*, houses were adorned with garlands,[237] Poppaea's and Nero's statues overthrown and some of those who had fallen from power were lynched.[238] Some of these manifestations were organized from above. They apparently served to advertise the high ideals and blessings of the new regime and, furthermore, to canalize and satisfy the public demand for revenge and redress: thus the bones of members of the imperial family who had been murdered were transferred to Augustus' mausoleum and their images were once more set up.[239] A dedication to *Libertas* is extant[240] and public executions of Nero's creatures were arranged and drew huge crowds; in this respect Galba did not, however, satisfy the populace: in all the theatres and the circus they demanded the execution of Tigellinus, but in vain.[241]

We are not told what was performed in the theatres on these occasions or in this period. Indeed we seldom are. Considering that Maternus in the mid seventies[242] was able to recite his "opposition" plays it is, however, difficult to see why an author whose play conformed so well with the official policy of the period should not have been granted at least the same possibilities.

Be this as it may: it is, I think, clear that the author did well in choosing the events in AD. 62 as the subject of his play. That year was a turning point. It saw the death of Burrus and retirement of Seneca, the execution of Plautus, Sulla and Octavia and what in retrospect could present itself as the prelude to the great popular revolt against Nero. Defamation has created in Nero a monster of apocalyptic dimensions. It is noteworthy, therefore, that this author concentrated on crimes which, in his analysis, were crimes against the people: the murders of those who enjoyed the *favor populi*, his hatred, and the fire, – whereas his chariots, Greek manners, and histrionic ambitions are conspicuously absent.[243] Those pursuits of Nero's were probably never as objectionable to the man in the street as to the upper classes.[244] Their absence form this catalogue of Nero's crimes may therefore indicate what sort of public the author – or those who commissioned the play – had in mind.

The divorce and marriage theme had the advantage of bringing the imperial *thalamus* and the role of its various occupants into focus: Messalina, Agrippina, Octavia, and Poppaea – the very names evoke the apocalyptic downfall of the dynasty. In its inverted form the motive did, moreover, enable the author to invest the wedding at the center of the play with an aura of preordained doom. An audience in AD. 68 would not be likely to overlook the political implications of the grand *fury-pronuba* scenes with their stress on future revenge; nor would they, when hearing her dream narrative, have forgotten that Octavia had been executed on the very day which, so recently, had seen the suicide of her murderer.[245]

Appendix I

A Note on Symmetry in the *Octavia*.

There are excellent observations on the symmetrical structure of this play in Lucas, Galliena, Herington (1961), and P.L. Schmidt. The fact that this author tends to distribute his lines in an ABA pattern does not, however, seem to have been observed before. There is to my knowledge nothing similar in Seneca's tragedies. These observations therefore seem to furnish yet another stylistic argument against the authenticity of the play.

There are two obvious examples: the Poppaea-*nutrix* scene which we have already discussed* and the Chorus-*nuntius*-Nero scenes which also have a center and two panels: the iambic panels 780-805 (chorus-*nuntius*) and 820-845 (Nero's monologue) both count 26 lines – and the report of the *nuntius* (792-805) is moreover of the same length as the center, an anapaestic chorus interlude (806-819) = 14 lines.

780-805		26	*Nuntius*-chorus
└──▶	792-805	(14)	*Nuntius*
806-819		14	Chorus
820-845		26	Nero

The iambic Seneca scenes exhibit a similar composition, but here there probably are some problems with the text:

Seneca's monologue	(377-437)	61
Nero/*praefectus* and Nero/Seneca	(437b-532)	96
Nero/Seneca	(533-592)	60

If one follows Delrius, Richter and Leo in deleting line 387b-388a – or, as I think one should, Ritter in deleting 388[246], the first panel is of the same length as the second. In the center a stress on symmetry can also be observed: first there are 25 lines, mainly with stichomythia (437b-461); then there are three speeches:

Nero	462-471	10
Seneca	472-491	20 (with a cut exactly in the middle[247])
Nero	492-532	41

---

* above p. 18.

This "doubling up" effect corresponds to the line of argument and it is, because of the uneven number in the third speech, tempting to regard the problems in the *locus vexatus* 516-7 as due to an interpolation rather than a lacuna.[248]

Be this as it may: it is noteworthy how well the author has succeeded in accomplishing the transitions between the first panel and the center – and the center and the second panel:
a) Seneca describes the Iron Age and the impending chaos – and Nero appears;
b) Nero rejects the *clementia* policy and speaks of the future of his House – and Seneca changes the subject:[249] throughout the second panel he tries to reconcile him with the imperiled Octavia. However, this panel differs from the center not only in its subject but also in the absence of numerical patterns and great speeches like those in the center.

The Octavia-*nutrix* scenes at the beginning of the play are similarly patterned. The two iambic speeches in the center both count 37 lines: 100-136 (Octavia) and 137-173 (*nutrix*). In the predominantly iambic second panel the editors have 99 lines whereas the figures vary – as could be expected – in the predominantly anapaestic first panel: Gronovius and Ballaira have 99 lines, Leo and Richter 100 (counting 99 twice) and Giardina 101 (counting 79 and 99 twice).

In the second panel only the nurse uses anapaests: her song has 21 lines (201-221). The lines which precede and follow it are all iambic: the panel opens with 15 lines, mainly with stichomythia (174-188) and 12 (189-200) with a long speech of the nurse – only interrupted once by a bitter aside from Octavia (195). After the song the lines are distributed in this manner: first Octavia answers the nurse with a magnificent imprecation of Nero (222-251) in 30 lines, the longest speech in the panel. Then there is another 21 lines of dialogue and the scene is over (252-272).

The first panel has only one iambic speech, the nurse's prologue (34-56). The scene opens with Octavia's monologue: she laments Messalina, Claudius and – after the nurse's prologue – Britannicus (1-33 and 57-71). At this point the first scene ends. The nurse joins Octavia and the rest of the panel is taken up with dialogue:

1. panel	1.sc.	Octavia's monologue nurse's prologue Octavia's monologue dialogue	1-33 34-56 57-71 72-99(a)	71	99/100/101
Center		Octavia nurse	100-136 137-173		2×37
2. panel		dialogue nurse's song Octavia's imprecation dialogue	174-200 201-221 (21) 222-251 (30) 252-272 (21)	72	99

It is tempting to go deeper into the problem as to how the monometra, to judge from this parameter, should be distributed. I shall however refrain from doing so here. Without a closer study of the distribution in the MSS than has hitherto been produced the element of circularity in the argument would become intolerable. It is to be hoped that someone will undertake such an analysis.

But the ABA patterning raises other problems as well: it involves more than half the lines of the play and does not seem to correspond to the rigid five act divisions of the play which have been suggested;[250] and what are the reasons for these patterns: purely aesthetic? or were they chosen for some scenic reason?

With Leo we may indeed conclude:

"Es ist offenbar, dass die Octavia nicht einzig von Seneca abhängig ist, sondern auf einen reicheren Vorrath an dramatischen Produkten und mannigfaltigere Abstufungen der Kunstform hinweist, als die Schablone Senecas erkennen lässt."[251]

Appendix II

Staging or recital? This is a complex question and has been much debated. I wish here to address myself only to those aspects which have a bearing on my argument.

In his chapter on *Unklare und wiedersprüchliche Angaben über den szenischen Rahmen* Zwierlein refers in passing to *Octavia* – and if we accept his criteria the verdict would apparently be that the play is *bühnenfremd* and therefore meant for recitation only.[252] I am not, however, sure that the difficulties which Zwierlein, and a number of other scholars, see in the first scene of the *Octavia* really are there.

Setting aside for the moment the arguments of Zwierlein, the problem boils down to the often repeated assertion: *der Ort der Handlung ist der Platz vor dem kaiserlichen Palaste in Rom.*[253] Hence the problems. In 72ff Octavia's nurse says:

"Vox en nostras perculit aures
tristis alumnae; cesset thalamis
inferre gradus tarda senectus?"

and she joins Octavia. If they join *in* the *thalamus* – and that is what the text seems to say – it would admittedly be highly unusual, and has therefore been doubted.[254] The alternative explanations are however unduly complicated and rather unconvincing. To me they all look like rather forced attempts to make the play conform to the scenic conventions with which these scholars apparently take it for granted that it *should* conform. Need I reiterate that nothing indicates that this author was expected to adhere strictly to the "rules"? There is no unity of time and place, there are two dream scenes and a ghost scene in the middle of the play. What is it, then, that makes this further deviation impossible? If, moreover, we assume – as most scholars do – that the play was meant for recitation the idea of an "in front of the palace" – scenery becomes odious. I seriously doubt that a Roman audience, at such a performance, would *imagine* their empress crying and discussing the agonies of her heart in the square in front of an imperial palace looking like the rear-wall of a contemporary theatre. Why should they, when the text is perfectly clear in suggesting that Octavia is in her *thalamus* and that Poppaea has just come out of it? And when the whole point of the two empress-*nutrix* scenes is that they take place in and in front of that sinister and symbolic chamber?

Apparently the objection that *eine Innenszene zu Beginn eines Stückes im antiken Drama unerhört wäre*[255] is relevant only if we assume that the play was actually staged. Zwierlein deserves praise for having made this perfectly clear. I have a feeling, however, that we know too little about this genre and the theatre of this period to determine whether or not it was indeed "unerhört" to stage such a scene. If literary conventions could be changed, so could scenic conventions; and Horace's very insistence on the "rules" surely indicates that reality was far more variegated than Horace wished – and Zwierlein will allow.

Be this as it may: in our interpretation we have deliberately allowed the question to remain *sub iudice* – but we have not, therefore, refrained from considering the play's dramatic effect. Recitals and staging have after all much in common. In either case the audience is expected to cooperate, whether in creating the relevant scenic framework for themselves, or in accepting the framework already there, primitive and unsatisfactory as it may be, as "the imperial *thalamus*" or "the square in front of the palace in Rome".

It is noteworthy how effective the *Octavia* is in some scenes, not only in suggesting such a framework, but also in investing the stage and scenery – and even the entries and exits – with a symbolic function. The drama makes possible the sort of interplay between visual and verbal signs that any director or duly responsive audience would appreciate. When for instance Octavia leaves her ancestral palace (646ff.) the stage and scenery greatly add to the effect of her words: she bids the Palace farewell – and the indignant chorus raises its call for attacking the *principis aulam* (690; cf. 668). Also here the stage, be it imaginary or not, has become a symbol.

In that scene Poppaea's triumph over Octavia finds visual

expression in the statues of herself at Nero's side; on seeing them (*en* 683) the indignant chorus expresses its wish that they be thrown over. Later, when the Poppaea chorus describes her fatal beauty ("vincet vultus haec Tyndaridos/qui moverunt horrida bella/Phrygiaeque solo regna dedere." 775-7) the messenger arrives and gives a vivid and detailed description of their actual overthrow.

The entries of Agrippina and of Nero are likewise well prepared for: the *fury-pronubae*, the Iron Age and the power of Cupid suddenly seem to take on a visual shape, as Agrippina and, in the two latter instances, as Nero (593ff; 436ff; 818ff.).

The author's tendency to contrast scenes (the two empress-*nutrix* and the two Nero-prefect scenes) and his manner of gradually removing Octavia, not only from the *thalamus* and her ancestral palace, but also, at her third appearance, from Rome itself also has considerable dramatic impact.

In the final embarkation scene Octavia *more vaticinantis* recognizes Agrippina's death ship in the ship that will take her to Pandateria – another dramatic effect for which we have been carefully prepared (906ff and 958ff; cf. 125ff; 310ff; 598ff).

Münscher – and others – here only sighted (*eine*) *leise Inkonzinnität:*

"freilich vor dem Kaiserpalast in Rom, vor dem das Stück *im übrigen* spielt, kann das Schiff *in Wahrheit* nicht sichtbar sein..." (my italics) – but those inconsistencies are, in my view, entirely of his own making.[256]

Appendix III

Apparently there is no reference in the *Octavia* to Otho, the paramour (or second husband?) of Poppaea.[257] One may speculate why: in the dream scene a reference to Otho would spoil the effective contrast between Poppaea's married life with Crispinus and her impious and criminal union with Nero – and it would likewise spoil the ambiguous murder-suicide scene.

The author could of course have referred to Otho in another context – and assuming that he wrote his play in the first years of the Flavians a reference to Otho's intimate connections with the *aula Neroniana* would probably be tolerable and perhaps even welcome;[258] if, on the other hand he wrote his play in the reign of Galba, references to Otho's liaison with Poppaea would probably be highly unpolitic. Otho had been quick to join Galba's cause; Galba was, for his part, apparently willing to forget that Otho had been intimate with the fallen tyrant[259] – many had – but it would probably not be wise to be too outspoken about it. Thus it was only when Galba had been murdered that Otho allowed himself – or found it expedient – to acknowledge his connection with Nero and Poppaea: among other things he saw to it that Poppaea's statues were restored.[260] The lack of reference to Otho is therefore perhaps another argument in favour of a Galban date.[261]

Manuscripts, editions, translations and literature referred to:

There are bibliographies on the *Octavia* in *Bursian* and *Lustrum* 2, 1957 (M. Coffey) and 9, 1964 (H.J. Mette) – and now also the thorough survey by P.L. Schmidt (to be published in the *ANRW*) which the author kindly has placed at my disposal and allowed me to quote.

The literature on the subject is vast and, at times, repetitive. In the notes I have therefore generally preferred to refer only to a few exponents of the relevant views.

The date of the *manuscripts* quoted is, if not otherwise indicated, that of the library catalogues.

As to the *editions of Seneca* which I have employed there is a survey, with all the bibliographical details, in Giardina p. xxxiff.

Where nothing else is indicated the *translations* and *separate editions* will be found under *Seneca* in the relevant bibliographies.

In the *list of literature referred to* I have employed the abbreviations of the *Oxford Classical Dictionary*.

Scholia from the following manuscripts:
London, British Library:
- Arundel 116 saec. XIV (Mac Gregor p. 328:XIV med?; its commentary was written "in apparent ignorance of Treveth's" by one "Francesco Ceccharelli (?: Lucharelli, Br. Mus. Catalogue) of Gubbio" (id. p.345).
- Harley 2484 saec. XIII (Philp p.153: "early fourteenth century"; MacGregor p.329: med. saec. XIV; "Its commentary acknowledges that of Treveth ... largely to disagree." id. p.347 note 29).
- Harley 2647 saec XV.
- Add. 17381 1475 (The text and the interlinear and marginal gloss are, according to Derolez p.39, written by one scribe).

Paris, Bibliothèque Nationale:
- 8030 saec. XV (Commentary partly from Treveth).
- 8035 saec. XV.
- 18547 saec. XIV.

The commentary of Treveth from 1315-16:
London, Society of Antiquaries 63 saec. XIV.
Paris, Bibliothèque Nationale 8032 saec. XV. (Palma p. xxxv: sec. XV in.).
                                                8038 saec. XV.

Editions, commentaries and early discussions of the text:
Hieronymus Avantius, *Emendationes tragoediarum Senecae.* Venice 1507.
Egidius Maseriensis, Paris 1511.
Iod. Badius Ascensius, Paris 1514.
Hieronymus Avantius, Venice 1517.
Justus Lipsius, *Animadversiones in tragoedias quae L. Annaeo Senecae tribuuntur*, Leiden 1588.
F. Raphelengius, Leiden 1589.
M.A. Delrius, Antverpen 1593.
J. Ġruterus, Heidelberg 1604.
(The edition Heidelberg 1600 I have not seen).
J. F. Gronovius, Leiden 1661.
F. Leo, Berlin 1878-9.
J.C. Giardina, Bologna 1966.

Translations and bilingual editions:
M.L. Dolce, Venice 1560.
*T. Nuce, London 1566.
R. Brisset, Tours 1590.
H. Nini, Venice 1622.
B. Bauduyn, Troyes 1629.
P. Linage, Paris 1651.
M. de Marolles, Paris 1660.
M.L. Coupé, Paris 1795.
W.A. Swoboda, Prag 1825-30.
J.-B. Levée, Paris 1822.
   (J.-B. Levée and Le Monnier, *Théâtre complet des latins*, vol 14)
M.E. Greslou, Paris 1834.
   (C.L.F. Panckoucke, *Bibliothèque latine-francaise*, vol 162)
M. Desforges, Paris 1850.
   (M. Nisard, *Collection des auteurs latins*, vol 1)

*A. Stahr, Agrippina, die Mutter Neros, Berlin 1867.
W. Bradshaw, London 1902.
*Octavia, en romersk tragedi, tolkad af F. Gustafsson, Helsingfors 1915.
F.J. Miller, Cambridge Mass, 1917 (Loeb).
*Ottavia, tragedia latina d'incerto autore ... ed. F. Ageno, Firenze 1920.
L. Herrmann, Paris 1926 (Budé).
*J. Köhm, Senecas Octavia und die Überlieferung von Neros Tod. *Festschrift d. 75.j. Best. des Röm.Germ. Central-Mus.* Mainz 1927.
M. Mignon, Paris 1935-37.
E. Paratore, Roma 1956.
T. Thomann, Zürich und Stuttgart 1961.
E.F. Watling, Four Tragedies and Octavia, (*Penguin Classics*) First publ. 1966.

*Only the *Octavia*.

Separate editions of the Octavia:
Octavia praetexta. Curiato Materno Vindicatam ...ed. F. Ritter, Bonn 1843.
A. Santoro, *Incerti poetae Octavia*. Bologna 1917.
C. Hosius, *Octavia praetexta cum elementis commentarii*, Bonn 1922.
G. Herzog-Hauser, *Octavia, fabula praetexta*, Wien/Leipzig 1934.
Th. H. Sluiter, *Octavia fabula praetexta*, Leiden 1949.
L. Pedroli, *Fabularum praetextarum quae extant*, Genova 1954.
La pretesta"*Octavia*" ed. P. Rizza. Messina – Firenze 1970.
G. Ballaira, Ottavia con note, Torino 1974.
L.Y. Whitman, The *Octavia*. Introduction, text and commentary. (*Noctes Romanae* 16, Bern, Stuttgart 1978)

References:
B. Axelson (review of Giancotti).
(*Gnomon* 28, 1956 p. 41ff)
H. Bardon, Notes sur la littérature impériale.
(*Latomus* 3, 1939 p. 250ff)
J. Béranger, Der *Genius populi Romani* in der Kaiserpolitik.
(*Bonner Jahrb.* 165, 1965, 72ff)

BMC British Museum Catalogue of Coins of the Roman Empire,
  London 1923–
T. Bollinger, *Theatralis licentia.* (Diss.)
  Winterthur 1969.
M.V. Bragington, The Supernatural in Seneca's Tragedies.
  Menasha, Wisconsin 1933.
F. Bruckner, Interpretationen zur Pseudo-Seneca-Tragödie *Octavia.* (Diss.) Nürnberg 1976.
P.A. Brunt, The Revolt of Vindex and the Fall of Nero.
  (*Latomus* 18, 1959, p.531ff)
M.E. Carbone, The *Octavia*: Structure, Date and Authenticity.
  (*Phoenix* 31, 1977, 48ff)
H. Chadwick, Gewissen.
  (*RAC* 10 coll. 1025ff)
G. Chalon, L'édit de Tiberius Julius Alexander.
  (*Bibliotheca Helvetica Romana* 5, Lausanne 1964)
M.P. Charlesworth 1936, *Providentia* and *Aeternitas.*
  (*Harvard Theological Review* XXIX, 1936 p.107ff)
M.P. Charlesworth 1937, *Flaviana.*
  (*JRS* 27, 1937, 54ff)
E.C. Chickering, An introduction to *Octavia Praetexta.*
  New York 1910.
M.H. Crawford, Roman Republican Coinage I-II.
  Cambridge 1974.
A. Derolez, The library of Raphael de Marcatellis. Ghent 1979.
P.J. Enk, *De Octavia praetexta.*
  (*Mnemos.* 54, 1926, 390ff)
A. Ferrill, Otho, Vitellius and the propaganda of Vespasian.
  (*CJ* 60, 1964-5 p.267ff)
E. Flinck, *De Octaviae praetextae auctore diss.* Helsingfors 1919.
W.H. Friedrich, Euripideisches in der lateinischen Literatur.
  (*Hermes* 69, 1934, 300ff)
H. Fuchs, Textgestaltungen in der Tragödie *Octavia.*
  (*Wien. Stud., Beiheft* 8, 1977, 71ff)
F. Fürbringer, *De somniis in Romanorum poetarum carminibus narratis diss.* Jena 1912.
J. Gagé, Vespasien et la mémoire de Galba.
  (*REA* 54, 1952, 290ff)

W. Galliena, La struttura simmetrica della *Octavia*.
(*Boll. Fil. Class.* 35, 1928-29, 304ff)

B. Gatz, Weltalter, goldene Zeit und sinnverwandte Vorstellungen.
(*Spudasmata* 16, 1967)

F. Giancotti, L'*Octavia* attribuita a Seneca.
Torino 1954.

J.-B. Giard, Le soulèvement de 68 et le réveil du monnayage local en Gaule.
(*Actes du 8 ème Congrès international de numismatique.* Paris 1976 p.279ff)

A.J. Greimas, Sémantique structurale. Paris 1966.

P. Hahlbrock, Beobachtungen zum jambischen Trimeter in den Tragödien des L. Annaeus Seneca.
(*Wien. Stud.* 81, *NF* 2, 1968, 171ff)

R. Helm 1934, Die *Praetexta 'Octavia'*.
(*Sitzb. d. preuss. Akad.* 1934, 283ff)

R. Helm 1954,*Praetexta*.
(*PW* 22.2 col. 1569ff)

C.J. Herington 1961, *Octavia Praetexta:* a Survey.
(*CQ* 11, 1961, 18ff)

C.J. Herington 1977, (review of Ballaira's ed.).
(*Gnomon* 49, 1977, 275ff)

T. Hermann, La tragédie nationale chez les Romains.
(*C&M* 9, 1947, 141ff)

L. Herrmann 1924, Octavie. Tragédie prétexte. Diss. Paris 1924.

L. Herrmann 1925, Octavie, source de Britannicus.
(*Bulletin Association G. Budé* nr. 7, 1925 p.15ff)

G. Herzog-Hauser, Reim und Stabreim in der praetexta *Octavia*.
(*Glotta* 25, 1936, 109ff)

L. Hjelmslev, Prolegomena to a theory of language.
(*Indiana University Publications in Anthropology and Linguistics*, Memoir 7. Baltimore 1953).

H.U. Instinsky, *Salus generis humani*.
(*Hamburger Beiträge zur Numismatik* 1, 1947 p.1ff)

R. Jakobson, Two types of language and two types of aphasic disturbancies.

(R. Jakobson and M. Halle, Fundamentals of language. Mouton, The Hague 1956 p.53ff)

E. Jockers, Die englischen Seneca-Uebersetzer des 16. Jahrhunderts. Diss. Strassburg 1909.

C.M. Kraay 1949, The coinage of Vindex and Galba, A.D. 68, and the continuity of the Augustan principate.
(*Num. Chron.* 1949, 129ff)

C.M. Kraay 1956, The *Aes* Coinage of Galba.
(*Numismatic Notes and Monographs*, 133, The American Numismatic Society, New York 1956)

C.M. Kraay 1978, The bronze coinage of Vespasian; classification and attribution.
(*Scripta nummaria Romana*. Essays presented to H. Sutherland, London 1978 p. 47ff)

P. Kragelund 1976, Dream and Prediction in the Aeneid.
(*Opuscula Graecolatina* 7, Copenhagen 1976)

P. Kragelund 1980, Antikke drømmeteorier – og Freuds.
(*Museum Tusculanum* 40-43, 1980, 365ff)

F. Ladek 1891, *De Octavia praetexta*.
(*Dissertationes philologicae Vindobonenses* III, Wien 1891)

F. Ladek 1905, Zur Frage über die historischen Quellen der *Octavia*.
(*Z. für die öst. Gym.* 1905, 673ff; 865ff; 961ff)

F. Ladek 1909, Die römische Tragödie *Octavia* und die Elektra des Sophokles.
(*Wiener Eranos* 1909, 189ff)

J. Lammers, Die Doppel – und Halbchöre in der antiken Tragödie. Diss. Paderborn 1931.

F. Leo, Die Composition der Chorlieder Senecas.
(*Rh.M* 52, 1897, 509ff)

F.L. Lucas, The *Octavia*.
(*CR* 35, 1921, 91ff)

J. Lyons, Semantics I-II. Cambridge 1977.

P. Maas, Die Prophezeiungen in Senecas *Octavia*.
(Kleine Schriften p. 606, München 1973)

A.P. MacGregor, The MS Tradition of Seneca's Tragedies: *Ante renatas in Italia Litteras*.
(*TAPA* 102, 1971, p.327ff)

R. MacMullen, Enemies of the Roman Order.
Treason, Unrest, and Alienation in the Empire.
Cambridge, Mass. 1966.

A. Marek, *De temporis et loci unitatibus a Seneca tragico observatis diss.*
Breslau 1909.

B. Marti, Senecas *Apocolocynthosis* and *Octavia*.
(*A.J.Ph.* 73, 1952, 24ff)

P.-H. Martin, Die anonymen Münzen des Jahres 68 n. Chr.
Mainz 1974.

H. Mattingly, The Coinage of the Civil Wars of 68-69 A.D.
(*Num. Chron.* 1914, 110ff)

K. Meiser, Ueber historische Dramen der Römer.
Festrede gehalten in d. öff. Sitz. d. k. Akad. d. Wiss. zu München.
München 1887.

H. Mende, De animarum in poesi epica et dramatica ascensu diss.
Breslau 1913.

G. Mickwitz, Tragedien *Octavia* och den tidigare *fabula praetexta*.
(*Eranos* XXVI, 1928, 234ff)

K. Münscher[a], Senecas Werke. Untersuchungen zur Abfassungszeit und Echtheit.
(*Philol., Suppl.* XVI. 1, Lpz. 1922)

K. Münscher[b], *Jahresb.* 192, 1922, 198ff.

J. Nicols, Vespasian and the *Partes Flavianae*.
(*Historia Einzelschriften* 28. 1978)

E.P. Nicolas, De Néron à Vespasien. Études et perspectives historiques. Paris 1979.

G. Nordmeyer, *De Octaviae fabula*.
(*Jahrb. f. cl. Phil., Suppl.* 19, 1893, 255ff)

M. Palma (ed.): N. Trevet, Commento alle *Troades* di Seneca.
(*Temi e Testi* 22, Roma 1977)

A.S. Pease 1919, Is the *Octavia* a play of Seneca?
(*CJ* 15, 1919-20, 388ff)

A.S. Pease 1924, The *Octavia* once more.
(*CPhil* 19, 1924, 80ff)

R.H. Philp, The Manuscript Tradition of Seneca's Tragedies.
(*CQ* 18, 1968 p.150ff)

L. v. Ranke, Die Tragödien Seneca's
(Sämmtliche Werke 51-2, Lpz 1888, 19ff)

RIC Roman Imperial Coinage ed. H. Mattingly and E.A. Sydenham, London 1923–

G. Runchina, Il prologo della pretesta *Octavia*.
(*Annali della fac. di magisterio di Cagliari, N.S.* 2, 1977-8, p.65ff)

Coluccio Salutati, Epistulario, vol. I.
(*Fonti per la storia d'Italia, Epistulari sec.* XIV, Roma 1891)

J. Schmidt, *Octavia*.
(*PW* 17.2, coll. 1788ff)

P.L. Schmidt, Die Poetisierung und Mythisierung der Geschichte in der Tragödie *Octavia*.
(To be published 1982; quoted by paragraph instead of page.)

P.H. Schrijvers, Die Traumtheorie des Lukrez.
(*Mnemos.* 33, 1980, 128ff)

H. Schwabl, Weltalter.
(*PW Suppl.* 15 coll. 783ff)

A. Siegmund, Zur Kritik der Tragödie *Octavia* II-III. Böhm-Leipa 1911.

R. Staehlin, Das Motiv der Mantik im antiken Drama.
(*RGVV* 12.1, 1912-13)

J.B. Stearns, Studies of the Dream as a Technical Device in Latin Epic and Drama. Diss. Lancaster 1927.

F. Stoessl, Prologos.
(*PW* 23.2 col. 2312ff)

P.L. Strack, Untersuchungen zur römischen Reichsprägung des zweiten Jahrhunderts I-III. Stuttgart 1931-37.

A.U. Stylow, *Libertas* und *liberalitas*. Diss. München 1972.

R. Syme, Tacitus I-II. Oxford 1958.

V. Sørensen, Seneca. Humanisten ved Neros hof. Copenhagen 1976.

S.P. Thomas, *De Octavia praetexta*.
(*Symb. Osl. 24, 1945, 48ff*)

TRF Tragicorum Romanorum Fragmenta. rec. O. Ribbeck, Lpz. 1897.[3]

W. Trillitzsch, Seneca im literarischen Urteil der Antike. Amsterdam 1971.

B.L. Ullmann, The Humanism of Coluccio Salutati.
(*Medioevo e umanesimo* 4, Padova 1963)

F. Vater, *Miscellaneorum criticorum fasciculus quintus*.
(*Jahrb. Suppl.* 19, 1853, 565ff)
J.P. Vernant, Tensions et ambiguïtés dans la tragédie grecque.
(J.P. Vernant and P. Vidal- Naquet, Mythe et tragédie en Grèce ancienne. Paris 1972 p. 19ff)
P. Werner, *De incendiis urbis Romae aetate imperatorum diss.* Lpz. 1906.
Z. Yavetz, *Plebs* and *princeps*. Oxford 1969.
O. Zwierlein 1966, Die Rezitationsdramen Senecas. Meissenheim 1966.
O. Zwierlein 1976, Versinterpolationen und Korruptelen in den Tragödien Senecas.
(*Würzburger Jahrbücher für die Altertumswissenschaft* 2. 1976 p.181ff)
O. Zwierlein 1979, Weiteres zum Seneca Tragicus (III)
(*Würzburger Jahrbücher für die Altertumswissenschaft* 5. 1979 p.163ff)
O. Zwierlein 1980, (Review of Whitman's ed.).
(*Gnomon* 52, 1980, 713ff)

Notes

1. An exception should be made for the articles by Herington (1961) and P. L. Schmidt and the dissertation of Bruckner.
2. Kragelund 1976.
3. Verg. *Aen.* 7.447ff; Luc. 3.11 and 15; Amm. Marc. 14.11,17; Claudianus, *de rap. Proserpinae* 3.79.
4. Lucr. 1.123(?); Verg. *G.* 1.477-8; Verg. *Aen.* 1.354; Ov. *Her.* 13.109; Ov. *Met.* 11.691; Val. Flac. 3.59; Apul. *Met* 8.8; Claudianus, *de raptu Proserpinae* III.88; *Orestis tragoedia* 524 (*PLM.* 5.55).
5. A wounded figure either predicts the misfortune of the dreaming person or others: Tib. II.6.37ff; Verg.*Aen*.2.268ff; Ov. *Fast.* 3.639ff and 5.457ff; Sil. *Pun*.2.561; Stat. *Theb.* 2.123-4; Tac. *Ann.* 1.65,2; *Orestis tragoedia* 524 (*PLM*.5.55); or it announces the misfortune, as in Accius, *Brutus* I.9 (*TRF.*) or the death of the person who appears in a wounded state in the dream, as in Verg. *Aen.* 1.353ff; Val. Max. I.vii, 8; *Octavia* 122; Val. Flac. I.47ff and 5.340; Suet. *Iul.* 81.3; Apul. *Met.* 1.18; 4.27 and 8.8.
6. Pacuvius, *Iliona* 4 (*TRF*) (= *Schol. Bob* in Cic. *Sest.* 59,126); Cic. *Div.* I. 28,59; Tib. II. 6.38; Verg. *Aen* 2.270 and 288; Sen. *Troades* 449; Luc. 3.10; *Octavia* 115; Sil. *Pun.* 8.166; Stat. *Theb.* 9.599; Stat. *Achil.* 1.132; Amm. Marc. 30.5,18; *Orestis tragoedia* 523 (*PLM* 5.55).
7. Verg. *Aen.* 2.272; Val. Max. I.7,7; Stat. *Theb.* 10.324-5; Suet. *Nero* 46; Cass. Dio 67.16; Cass. Dio 75.8 (from a Latin source); Claudianus, *de raptu Proserpinae* III.72 and 87.
8. Verg. *Aen.* 2.289; Luc. 3.11; Stat. *Theb.* 8.631 and 9.582.
9. Ennius (?) *sc.* 35 (Vahlen); cf. Lactantius Placidus *ad* Stat. *Achil.* 1.22; Verg. *Aen.* 7.456; Ov. *Her.* 16.46; Luc. 7.772; *Octavia* 118.
10. *Schol. Bob. in* Cic. *pro Sest.* 59,126; Verg. *Aen.* 2.277; Ov. *Fas.* 3.640; Val. Max. I.7,7; Sen. *Troades* 450; *Quintiliani quae feruntur decl maior* 10 (ed. Lehnert) p.202.16; Amm. Marc. 30.5,18; Claudianus, *de raptu Proserpinae* 3.86.
11. Stat. *Theb.* 9.595ff; Tac. *Ann.* 2.14,1; Cf. note 5.
12. Cic. *Div.* I.28,58; Verg. *Aen.* 4.353; Verg. *Aen.* 7.446; Ov. *Fast*.3.36; Luc. 3.35; Luc. 7.764; Val. Flac. 5.232; Val. Flac. 5.335ff; Val. Flac. 7.143.
13. Ennius, *Ann.* 40 (Vahlen); Cic. *Div*.I.28.59; Verg. *Aen.* 4.466-8; Apul. *Met.* 4.27; SHA. *Sev.* 22.2.
14. Accius, *Brutus* I. 8-9 (*TRF*); Cic. *Div*.I. 28.58; Stat. *Theb.* 9.581; Suet. *div. Iul.* 81,3; Suet. *Galig.* 57.3; Cass. Dio 67,16; Herodian II.9,6; SHA. *Sev.* 22.2.
15. Accius, *Brutus* I. 11-12. (*TRF*); Verg. *Aen.* 2.281; Verg. *Aen.* 2.285; Verg. *Aen*.3.151; Ov. *Met.* 9.689; Val. Flac. 1.301; cf. *ibid.* 309; Apul. *Met.* 11.3ff; Suet. *Aug.* 94,6; Amm. Marc. 21.2,2.
16. Accius, *Brutus* I.4 (*TRF*); Tac. *Ann.* 2.14,1; Suet. *Aug.* 94.9.
17. Cic. *Div.* I. 28.58; Suet.*Aug.* 94.4; SHA. *Sev.* 22.1-2; SHA. *Sev. Alex* 14.2; Herodian II.9,6.
18. Cf. notes 4(?); 5; 6; 9; 10(?); 13; 14; 15; 16; 17.

19. Cf. note 3; 9; 11.
20. Cf. note 6.
21. Probably also a conventional sign of misfortune. Cf. Verg. *Aen.* 4.465-6 "*agit ipse furentem/in somnis ferus Aeneas..*" and Suet. *Ner.* 46 "vidit (sc. Nero) per quietem ... trahi ... se ab Octavia uxore in artissimas tenebras".
22. Cf. note 12.
23. Cf. note 14.
24. Cf. Cass. Dio 67.16; in Pompey's dream in Lucan's *Pharsalia* 3.9ff Iulia emerges from Hades through such an abyss:
 "Diri tum plena horroris imago/visa caput maestum per hiantes Iulia terras/ tollere et accenso furialis stare sepulcro."
25. Cf. for instance *Octavia* 593ff.
26. Cf. note 5.
27. "coniugis" 739.
28. For a full survey of the discussion: Giancotti 28-46 and the ed. of Ballaira *ad loc.*
29. An early exponent of this view is Ascensius (1514), but the idea is apparently older than that: the glosses in the MS of the abbé Raphael de Marcatellis (British Library add. 17.381 – the date of which appears to be 1475 (Derolez p.25: between 1463 and 78) – seem to take the same stand.
 Among the scholars who have held this view in recent years are:
 Ritter *ad loc.*; Nordmeyer p.267-8; Staehlin p.167; Santoro *ad loc.*; Pease 1919 p.392-3; Lucas p.92; Pease 1924 p.81; Bragington p.95; Bardon p.257; Giancotti p.44; Rizza p.43; P.L. Schmidt, III.
 Of these scholars Pease and Giancotti regarded the play as genuine, whereas Bardon suggested Lucan wrote it.
30. Tac. *Ann.* 16.17.
31. The idea that the play hints at Nero's actual manner of death goes, to our knowledge, back as far as to Coluccio Salutati's (p.152) remarks on the ghost scene in his famous letter from 1371. The letter was apparently widely circulated (Ullmann p.21 and 98). There are copies of it in some MSS of the tragedies and there are glosses like "suo", "suo proprio", "suomet" (*sc.* "iugulo") and "Neronis" or "Neronis se ipsum iugulantis" (to "coniugis" 739) in some of the MSS in the British Library (Arundel 116; Harley 2647 and Harley 2484) and in the Bibliothèque Nationale (8030; 8035 and 18547) which I have inspected. As for the age of these scholia I am no qualified judge, but the problem has been discussed at least since Treveth who, in his influential commentary from 1315-16, settled on "suo". Apparently Treveth failed to see the chronological implications, but his quotation from Eutropius XV *ad* 620ff may well have made people start wondering...
 Modern scholars who have held this view include:
 Vater p.598-9; Chickering p. 73; Herrmann 1924 p.7; Enk p.395; Helm p.294; Pedroli *ad loc*; Bruckner p.6; Carbone p.64; Zwierlein 1980, 716 – and also Ranke p.65 who, however, deems the dream too inaccurate to depict Nero's actual manner of death.
32. Lucr. 4.1014; Stat. *Theb.* 2.123; Apul *Met.* I.18.

33. 733. Cf. 530-1 and 796-7.
34. Cf. note 12.
35. Flinck p.7: "Hoc utut est, et ego quidem nescio an rectius ex sententia *suo* iugulo addatur, certum est tam obscura esse verba somniantis, ut nihil, quod ad res gestas in Octavia non commemoratas pertineat, ex iis elicere possit interpres.";
Herzog-Hauser *ad* 739: "Der Ausdruck ist unklar; es ist wohl an Nero's Selbstmord gedacht.";
Thomas p.79: "Sic sive Crispinum intellegimus sive Neronem interpretatio dubitationi obnoxia est";
Maas p.606 simply states that the text is ambiguous; Schmidt coll. 1793, Sluiter p.18 and Ballaira and Whitman *ad loc.* take the same stand.
36. Cf. Ladek 1891 p.6 and 1905,868 note 1.
37. Münscher[a] p.128 note 1; Münscher[b] p.203.
38. Cf. the list of translations which I have consulted. Indications of doubt are seldom found in these translations. Ageno is, it is true, ambiguous in his translation of 752 (cf. Giancotti p.42 and Ballaira *ad loc.*) but *not* in 733, where Crispinus is said to be the victim. Desforges (p.211) admitted that "ce vers est ... susceptible de diverses interprétations" but Swoboda assures us that "dies ist meines Bedünkens die einzig richtige Deutung dieser Stelle..." (Bd. III p.372).
39. Thomann Bd. I p.502; 535; 553.
40. Köhm did likewise. As for his reasons for doing so cf. note 63.
41. Flinck p.44; Helm p.317; Hahlbrock p.191:
"Während in allen übrigen untersuchten Dramen diese (Personal- und Possessiv-) Pronomina zwischen 4,8% (Phaedra) und 13,2% (Hercules Oetaeus) der zweisilbigen Schlusswörter ausmachen, nehmen sie in der Octavia 22,5% ein."; Carbone's suggestion (p. 59) that the obscurity of the dream is due to this tendency is, as should be apparent, selfcontradictory.
42. Cic. *Div.* I.18,34; II.64,131.
43. In dreams:
numerals: Verg. *Aen.* 8.44; Suet. *Vesp.* 25;
puns: Accius, *Brutus* II.4 (*TRF*);
Apuleius *Met.*11.20; 11.27;
Cass. Dio 75.8;
ambiguities: Soph.*El.* 410ff;
Eur. *IT.* 42ff;
Ov. *Her.*16. 41ff; cf 17. 237ff;
Curtius Rufus 3.3.4;
App. *BCiv.* 2.68-9;
Claudianus, *in Ruf.* II. 327ff.
44. Cf. Stat. *Theb.* 9.622 "Quid trepidae noctes somnusque minantur?" (concerning a dream). Similarly Ov. *Met.* 9.495 and Stat. *Theb.* 8.633.
Like Poppaea Aeneas and Laodamia ask what specific signs mean: Verg. *Aen.* 2.286: "...cur haec *vulnera* cerno?" and Ov. *Her.* XIII,109-10: "Sed tua cur nobis *pallens* occurrit imago?/Cur venit a verbis multa *querella* tuis?".

45. husbands 729ff; wedding 718ff; bed 726-8.
46. Cf. the diviner in Accius' *Brutus:* first some general reflections on the nature of dreams, then a discussion of some of its features according to the order in which they occur in the dream. The latter was apparently the traditional way of structuring the interpretation in such scenes: Ov. *Am.* 3,5; Curtius Rufus 3.iii,4; Plut. *de Gen.*(*mor.*587); an exception: *Querolus* 24ff (ed. Randstrand).
47. Nordmeyer p.267; Whitman repeats Nordmeyer's arguments, but in her comments to 732 and 752 she leaves the question open.
48. Helm p.294.
49. "praelata" 749.
50. Being the product of fire light easily lends itself to a negative interpretation: cf. for instance the false interpretation of the expression "magno ignis fulgore conlucere" in Dareius' dream, Curtius Rufus 3.iii,3.
51. Fuchs p.76.
52. Thomas p.79-80.
53. Justus Lipsius *ad* 752: "Malo "princeps tuo"".
54. Raphelengius *ad* 732: (First he discusses Lipsius' suggestion) "Proba ista lectio, probata nempe a Lipsio ... Malebam ego "tum trepidus, meo"...".
55. Hosius *in app. crit. ad loc.*
56. Lipsius *ad* 732: "Malo "trepidus meus" de Nerone".
57. Delrius *ad* 732: "Mallem "meus" si quis liber confirmaret. Suum vocat Neronem.".
58. Gruterus *ad* 732: "Ceterum si vox ultima reformanda esset, mallem "meo" quam "mea" ... immo potius scripserim "cum trepidus Nero/ensemque iugulo condidit saevum meo".
59. Raphelengius *ad* 752.
60. Gruterus *ad* 752: "Non male qui postremam mutant in "tuo". Solum miror, cur heic illud "tuus" excludant, cum tamen ambitiose supra intrusum voluerint "meus Nero". Nam ita sane loquuntur mulieres, apud Plautum, apud Terentium.".
61. It was, however, accepted in the translations of Bauduyn(?), Coupé and Levée and in the diss. of Fürbringer p.35.
62. Gronovius *ad* 732: "At, o boni, his omnibus quem redditis in illa nocturna imagine saucium? Annon Poppaeam? Cur ergo dicit ipsa 'aut quem cruorem coniugis vidi mei?' Non suum, sed coniugis cruorem se vidisse ait. Ergo aut Crispini aut Neronis." (Gronovius opted for Nero).
63. Maas p.606; accepted by Ballaira *ad loc.* Köhm argues along the same lines: p.229 and 250. Similarly Schmidt coll. 1793, Sluiter p.18 and Whitman *ad loc.*
64. Herington 1961 p.21.
65. 123ff and 734ff; cf. Galliena p.309.
66. 120; in Poppaea's infernal "thalamus" ("tecta..mea" 732) she finds her marriage couch ("toros/cerno iugales pariter et miror meos" 726-7).
67. 120 "trepidus" (Britannicus), 724 "coacta praesenti metu" (Poppaea), 732 "trepidus" (Nero).
68. "ensem" 122 and 733: in either case in the final line. It is, therefore, misleading in my view to speak of the "few similarities" between these dreams (Carbone

p.60). Indeed the presence of two dreams in one tragedy is in itself something unique (Staehlin p.170) which demands closer scrutiny.
Bragington explains it – unconvincingly – as due to the "author's tendency to bring in the supernatural at every opportunity" (p.95).
69. For a discussion of some of the material: Kragelund 1980.
70. Luc. 7.7ff; Lucr. 4.1024ff; Ov. *Met.* 8.823ff and 9.468ff; Hor. *Serm.* I.5.82ff; *PLM* 4.103; *AP* 12.125.
71. Cic. *Div.* II.68.140.
72. Cic. *Div* I.28.58.
73. Verg. *Aen.* 12.908ff.
74. Tib. Claudius Donatus *ad loc. cit.*
75. Hor. *carm.* 4.1.37ff.
76. Lucr. 4.1097ff.
77. Stat. *Theb.* 7.463ff.
78. Ennius *Ann.* 42-3 (Vahlen); Verg. *Aen.* 4.466-8.
79. Ennius *Ann.* 42-3 (Vahlen).
80. Porphyrion *ad* Hor. *carm.* 4.1.37ff.
81. Lucr. 3. 112ff; Ov.*ex Ponto* I, 2.43 and 51; Stat. *Theb.* 7.463ff; Macr. *Somn. Scip.* I.3,4.
82. Cf. Luc. 7.7ff; Curtius Rufus 3.3.2; Ov. *Her.* 13. 103ff; Cic.*Div.* I.28.58 and II 68.140; Stat. *Theb.* 8.623ff; Verg. *Ecl.* 8.108 and *Octavia* 740-42.
83. Val. Flac 4.38ff.
84. Jockers p.76 was puzzled by Nuce's tendency to translate *thalamus* as *thewes* or *thews* (73; 120; 276). But living in a society where social status often was indicated in a similarly symbolic manner Nuce would readily understand that this author sometimes means *might* or *strength* when he speaks of her *thalamus*.
85. 657; 671.
86. 909-10; 891ff: modo cui patriam/reddere cives aulam et fratris/voluere toros, nunc ad poenam/letumque trahi flentem miseram/cernere possunt.
87. 131ff: inimica victrix imminet thalamis meis/odioque nostri flagrat et pretium stupri/iustae maritum coniugis poscit caput.
88. 671ff: cessit thalamis Claudia diri/pulsa Neronis quos iam victrix/Poppaea tenet.
89. 688: ipsamque (sc. Poppaeam) toris detrahat altis.
90. 754-55: Recollige animum, recipe laetitiam, precor,/timore pulso redde te thalamis tuis.
91. Cf. note 6.
92. Cf. Hor. *carm.* 4.1,38: "*iam* captum teneo, *iam* volucrem sequor" and Stat. *Theb.* 7.463ff: "Si tenuis demisit lumina somnus/ bella gerunt; *modo* lucra morae, *modo* taedia vitae/ attonitis, lucemque timent lucemque precantur."
For a discussion of semantic field theory cf. for instance Lyons p.250ff and Greimas p.69ff.
93. 120 "trepidus".
94. 120 "refugit".
95. 121 "persequitur".
96. Cf. Ballaira *ad loc.*

97. Helm p.288 note 1. He suggested to read *strictum* instead of *nostrum*.
98. "...die Andeutungen über Octavias Tod (sind) nur vage oder sogar falsch ..., denn nach den Traumgesichten v.115ff sollte man eigentlich annehmen, Octavia wäre von Nero mit dem Schwerte getötet worden ..." Schmidt col. 1793.
99. Curtius Rufus 3.3.4; Ov. *Her.* 16.41ff; cf. 17.237ff; Soph. *El.* 410ff; App. *BCiv.* 2.68-9; Claudianus, *in Ruf.* II.327ff; Eur. *IT.* 42ff.
   On ambiguity in greek tragedy see Vernant 1972 p.35ff.
100. Mommsen, *Röm. Staatsrecht* I. 434.
101. Tac. *Hist.* III. 68,2.
102. Nordmeyer 311ff; Gatz 136ff.
103. Calpurnius Siculus I.63.
104. Sen. *Clem.* I.1,3.
105. Sen. *Clem.* I.11,3.
106. 456: "Ferrum tuetur principem". Bruckner p.52 rightly calls the sword a keyword; cf. P.L. Schmidt III.
107. 461 + "despectus ensis faciet"; various remedies have been suggested: Raphelengius "Destrictus ensis faciet" is, in my view, the most attractive.
108. 440ff: SEN "Nihil in propinquos temere constitui decet."
   NER "Iustum esse facile est cui vacat pectus metu."
   SEN "Magnum timoris remedium clementia est."
   NER "Extinguere hostem maxima est virtus ducis."
   Cf. Bruckner p.52ff. on the fear motive.
109. 457: NER "Decet timeri Caesarem" SEN "At plus diligi"
   NER "Metuant necesse est –"
110. 526 (Watling).
111. Britannicus is "trepidus" 120; Octavia wakes up in fear 123-4.
112. 544: "dignamque thalamis coniugem inveni meis".
113. 592: "Quin destinamus proximum thalamis diem?"
114. Cf. Sen. *Thyestes* 1ff and *Agamemnon* 1ff. The occurrence of a ghost scene in the middle of a play is apparently something unique: Mende p.44.
115. von Ranke p.65: "Selbst was von dem unglücklichen Ende Neros gesagt wird, ist zu allgemein, als dass es der Prophezeiung vorausgegangen sein könnte."; Similarly Siegmund p.20ff; Pease 1919 p.389ff; Thomas 67ff; Marti 26; Ballaira *ad* 629ff.
116. Ladek 1891 p.5; Münscher[b] p.204ff; Helm 1934 p.291ff; Herrmann 1924 p.8 justly speaks of an "inexactitude relative"; cf. id. p.10.
117. Flinck p.6; Thomas p.71; Enk. p.393.
118. Siegmund p.22ff.
119. Cf. note 115.
120. There is a sound discussion of the ghost scene in Carbone p.50ff.
121. Helm 1934 p.313 pointed out that *thalamus* occurs far more often in the *Octavia* than in any of Seneca's tragedies and that this author does not have the synonyms *nuptiae; coniugium; connubium*. The reason probably is that none of these words had similar polysemic advantages.
122. Cf. Ov. *Her.* 2.117; 6.45ff; 11.103ff; *Met.* 6.428ff.

123. Ov. *Her.* 12.140ff.
124. Ov. *Her.* 14.31ff; Sen. *Controv.* 6.6.
125. An instance of *species pro specie;* on metonymy cf. Jakobson p.76ff.
126. Herington 1961 p.22; a number of scholars, among them Fuchs p.72, assign the dream scene to the day of the wedding, but cf. P.L. Schmidt, IV (with previous literature).
127. 693ff: "Certe petitus precibus et votis dies/nostris refulsit: Caesari iuncta es tuo/taeda iugali".
128. 708 "quorum toros celebrasse caelestes ferunt".
129. 718-9; *celebrare* may designate weddings as well as funerals: *TLL* III 743.64ff and 744.54ff.
130. It is not correct that the connection between ghost scene and dream has been observed only in "a very few earlier studies" (Carbone p.60). To his list could be added Ladek 1909 p. 194-5; Staehlin p.167^2; Lucas p.93; Mickwitz p.240; Köhm p.229; Stearns p.38 and Axelson p.42.
131. I fear that Whitman, who argues (*ad* 732) that the *torus* is "not in the underworld", has missed the whole point of the scene.
132. 719 "resolutis comis"; as to the presence of "matres Latinae" at an imperial funeral cf. *Consolatio ad Liviam* 203ff:
"Omnis adest aetas maerent iuvenesque senesque/Ausoniae matres Ausoniaeque nurus."
133. 720 "flebiles planctus".
134. 721 "inter tubarum ... sonum".
135. In dreams: Luc. 7.760ff and *Adnotationes super Lucanum* (ed. Endt) *ad* 7.784; Amm. Marc. 14.11.17. Cf. Chadwick coll. 1038-9; Schrijvers p.147.
136. 724 "sequor coacta praesenti metu".
137. Cf. Cat. 61.159; Luc. 2.359.
138. Cf. Donatus *ad* Ter. *Eun.* 593.
139. 728 "in quis residi fessa".
140. Cf. Cat. 61.184ff: "Iam licet venias, marite:/uxor in thalamo tibist," and Petron. *Sat.* 26 (a parody).
141. 728ff; the reading *Crispinus* is not – as indicated by e.g. Leo, Peiper-Richter and Giardina – due to Avantius. In 1507 Avantius, if I understand him correctly, argued in favour of *pristinus*. It was Aegidius Maser (1511) who, in a note, suggested *Crispinus*. Ascensius (1514) was full of compliments, but did not approve, whereas Avantius, in 1517, accepted the reading in his text.
142. 729; in dreams solitude is, as we have seen, a sign of misfortune (cf. note 13) whereas the opposite seems to indicate something favourable – not surprisingly, considering the social status which it often connotes: Cic. *Div.* I.28.59; Ov. *Met.* 9.687 and SHA. *Sev.* 22.2.
143. Cf. 703ff "Et ipse lateri iunctus atque haerens tuo/sublimis inter civium laeta omina/incessit habitu atque ore laetitiam gerens/princeps superbo...".
144. Cf. note 68.
145. Cf. note 67.
146. 760-1; *status* Buecheler, *metus codd.*
147. The double dream scenes in Ar. *Hipp.* 1090ff. and *Vesp.* 10ff. may of course be

a parody of similar tragic scenes. The influence from Euripides' *Hecuba* on Poppaea's dream is evident, but I cannot follow Friedrich p.313 who detects an influence from "Urphaedra".
148. Verg. *Aen.* 2.270ff and 7.415ff; these dreams have the following formal properties in common:

I Description of the dream figure:	2.270-280 and 7.415-420
II Dialogue:	2.281-295 and 7.421-455
III Dream figure's gesture:	2.296-297 and 7.456-457
IV Concluding simile:	2.304-308 and 7.462-466

Cf. Kragelund 1976 p.63ff. As for Vergil's manner of introducing Aeneas and Turnus I was mistaken when stating that "Turnus has been mentioned only once before" (*ibid.* p.72) – which does not, however, invalidate the argument: that it is in the dream scene that Turnus is introduced and involved in the action, exactly as is the case with Aeneas, in his retrospective narration.
Statius introduced Eteocles in a similar manner:
I: *Theb.* 2.94-101; II: 2.102-119; III: 2.120-124; IV: 2.128-133 alluding above all to Turnus' nightmare (Laios' metamorphosis!). It should be noted, however, that there is no dialogue in II.
In Lucan the vision of Caesar (1.186ff) and the dream of Pompey (7.1ff) are apparently also meant as a pair. It is, however, only Caesar's vision which exhibits formal properties similar to those of Vergil's introductory dreams:
I:1.186-190; II: 1.190-203; III: 1.204-205 (The gesture is Caesar's!); IV: 1.205-212 – and it is again the dream of Turnus, with its stress on his egotism (cf. Kragelund 1976 p.72ff) which has exerted the major influence. As in Vergil, the simile has a prophetic quality: it forebodes the fate of the victorious Caesar. The dream of Pompey which opens the 7th book has, moreover, a Caesarian counterpart at the end of that book: 7.764ff.
149. Ladek 1909, 195.
150. Accius, *Brutus* II.8ff (*TRF*).
151. Chickering p.74; also Vater p.599; cf. Accius, *Brutus* II 5ff (*TRF*); Ov. *Fas.* 3.27ff; Ov. *Am* 3.5; Val. Flac. 5.334ff; Curtius Rufus III.3.4.
152. Cf. the interpretation of *manifesta fides* Verg. *Aen.* 2.309 in Kragelund 1976, 41-2; I had overlooked *manifesta fide* (of a dream) in *Querolus* 25.4 (ed. Randstrand).
153. Sørensen p.306.
154. Sen. *Clem.* I.12,4 and 25,3.
155. Thus the *communis opinio;* against Lammers p.137ff (with previous literature) according to whom "(diesem) Chor ...(e.g. the latter)... jegliche characteristische Unterscheidung von dem andern abgeht" (p.138[8]), but later Herzog Hauser pointed out the differences in style (p.113). There is, furthermore, the content: the Octavia chorus "represents" the people and shares its attitudes; it is consistent in referring to the republican past (288ff; 676ff; 882ff); they speak of " us" and "our city" (288; 674; 979); note also that Octavia speaks to the chorus of their "amor" and "favor" (647-8), the messenger of the people (781; 802) and its "favor" (786; 792) and the chorus again of "populi/ ...favor (877-8) and "plebis amor/nimiusque favor" (883-4) – the other chorus does no such

thing: it addresses the rioting people with reproof (806; 808; 811-2). It should be noted, finally, that the words of the Poppaea chorus are opposed to the ideal of chastity cherished by the following and allies of Octavia: thus the former's praise of Iuppiter's immoral affairs is strongly at variance with the way in which Octavia's nurse refers to the "furta Iovis" (762ff; 201ff); likewise with their praise of Cupid – as compared to the Octavia chorus' and Seneca's praise of her chastity (807ff; 287; 539; 587) – and the latter's rejection of "Amor" (553ff).

It has also been argued that the chorus in the final scene is identical with the Poppaea chorus (Herington 1961 p.22[5] and (?) 1977 p.278; now also P.L. Schmidt, III). The argument overlooks the striking similarities between the ideological stance of the Octavia chorus and the chorus in the final scene: one instance is the positive attitude towards everything republican; another is their moral outlook: thus the Octavia chorus is confident that her offspring will be "pignora pacis" (279) and the chorus in the final scene praises Agrippina maior in a similar manner: "...cuius nomen/clarum toto fulsit in orbe/ utero totiens enixa gravi/*pignora pacis* ..." (935-8); there is, furthermore, their attitude towards Nero: both choruses condemn Nero's murder of Agrippina: "Haec quoque nati videre nefas/ saecula magnum ..." (310-11) and "mox et ferro lacerata diu/*saevi* iacuit victima *nati*" (956-7) – the latter are hardly words to expect from Poppaea's courtiers; and finally there is the immoral attitude of her court – an attitude completely incompatible with the stoicism of the chorus in the final scene.

Too much has been made of the difficulty in 892-5 where the chorus speaks of the "cives" in the third person; Giardina's solution, "possis" (895) does not, it is true, recommend itself, but sudden changes from the first to the third person are not without parallels in the chorus scenes of this play: consider, for instance "nostra" (674) and then "Romani ...populi" (676) and then again "nostris" (683) – or, in the final scene, "precor" (978), "urbe ... nostra" (979) and then, suddenly, "*civis* gaudet Roma cruore" (983). In either case the expression would loose its poignancy if the chorus had said "nostra" or "nostro", but nothing indicates that the chorus speaks of a body totally different from – or even opposed to – itself. Likewise in 892-5 – where it should be understood that the chorus speaks, *not* so much of the "unreliability of mob-support" (Herington 1961 p.22[5]) – in this play it is only Nero and the messenger who refer to the "populus" in depreciatory terms like "vulgus" or "(corrupta) turba" (455: 579: 796: 835: 851) or even "ministros sceleris" (466) – as of the *citizens'* deplorable lack of power to support its champions (cf. 675 where they speak of their "segnis... dolor" and 288: "Nos quoque nostri sumus immemores...").

156. 300 "victrix ... libido".
157. Livy I. 58.5 ("victrix libido"); 59.8; 3.44; 44.2; 48; 50.9.
158. Lammers' comments on the chorus are misleading: "Immer wird von anderen geredet, die etwas ausgerichtet haben oder ausrichten sollen; selbst zeigt der Chor Passivität." (p.137). Herrmann 1924 rightly emphasized the activity of the chorus and its decisive influence on the cause of events – as compared with

the traditional Senecan chorus (p.151); the active role of the people of Rome in Racine's *Britannicus* may well owe something to the *Octavia*: Herrmann 1925 p.18.
159. Cf. Ranke p.63: "...die Verflechtung liegt darin, dass die Legitimität, als deren Vertreterin Octavia erscheint, zugleich populär ist, und die Frechheit des Fürsten, der sich über die Gesetze erhebt, seine eigene Macht in Gefahr bringt."
160. Tac. *Ann.* 14.60,5 "Inde crebri questus nec occulti per vulgum, cui minor sapientia <et> ex mediocritate fortunae pauciora pericula sunt" – *e.q.s.*
161. For the sources see Werner p.20.
162. 831ff; 857; "in Octavia Neronem propter favorem populi erga Octaviam urbem delendam esse constituere, apud historicos alias afferri causas, luxuriam et magnificentiam." Nordmeyer 266. Likewise Ladek 1905, 696 and 699.
    Tacitus does, however, record popular rumours and hostility: *Ann.* XV. 39,3; 40,2; 44,5; and to judge from the cryptic "sed nec *populo* aut moenibus patriae pepercit" Suetonius may have known a similar version (Suet. *Ner.* 38; cf. the rumours in 43).
    Poppaea's contemptuous description of Octavia's supporters: "clientelis et servitiis Octaviae, quae plebis sibi nomen indiderint" (*Ann.* 14.61,2) may furthermore indicate that Tacitus was acquainted with a tradition according to which it was a mob parading as the people – or simply the people – which had rioted on behalf of Octavia.
163. Trillitzsch p.48.
164. Nordmeyer 308-9.
165. Nordmeyer 288; Herington 1961 p.28-9.
166. Thus the *communis opinio:* Ladek 1891 p.7ff and Bruder p.7 (both with previous lit.); see also Chickering p.83ff; Enk p.415; Lucas p.92; Carbone p.67. The attempts to determine the priority of the *Octavia vis-à-vis* Tacitus have, in my view, led to nothing certain.
167. Challenging the interpretation originally suggested by Mattingly in 1914, Martin has convincingly argued "dass alle anonymen Münzen ihre Entstehung im Umkreis Galbas haben" (p.46). In what follows I shall discuss the numismatic evidence on the assumption that this interpretation is correct. To faciliate comparison I shall, however, indicate whenever one of the coins under discussion belongs, according to the *RIC.* to the so-called Military class or the coinage of Civilis. As for the so-called Gallic coinage of Vindex, I have not deemed it necessary for the present purpose: Vindex and Galba did, after all, soon become allies.
168. Suet. *Galba* 10; Plut. *Galba* 5.
169. *BMC.* I p.272 and 275 (P.R); p.268; 271; 273; 275 (S.P.Q.R); cf. Giard p.284-5.
170. *BMC.* I p.cxc.
171. Mattingly 117; Kraay 1949,135.
172. The coins with this legend are in the *RIC.* all assigned to the "military" class, but cf. note 167.
173. *BMC.* I p.cxcii.

174. Martin p.54; Strack II.98.
175. Plut. *Galba* 4; Nero's party also had their songs: Suet. *Nero* 42.2; Suet. *Nero* 41; Suet. *Galba* 10.3.
176. Suet. *Nero* 45.2. The story in Tacitus of the dagger which Nero dedicated to Iuppiter Vindex: "in praesens haud animadversum post arma Iulii Vindicis ad auspicium et praesagium futurae ultionis trahebatur." (*Ann.* 15.74,2) might be contemporary; likewise the observation that Vindex' rebellion coincided with the anniversary of Agrippina's death: Suet. *Nero* 40.4.
177. Donatus *ad* Ter. *Ad.* 194: "Assertores dicuntur vindices alienae libertatis".
    Galba "humano generi assertorem" Suet. *Galba* 9.2.
    Vespasian "ADSERTORI LIBERTATIS PUBLIC (AE)." *RIC.* II 65 nr. 411; *ibid.* 70 nr. 455 and 456 (70-71 AD).
    Vindex "adsertorem illum a Nerone libertatis" Plin.*NH*.20.160. Cf. Kraay 1949,139.
    Later, Martial called the year 68 AD "sacer": it saw the liberation of the world ("adserto.. orbe" 7.63.10). He spoke also of Domitianus as the "adsertor" of the Palace (from Vitellius): "Adseruit possessa malis Palatia regnis" 9.101.13. The epitaph of Verginius Rufus still echoes the slogans of the civil wars – with a very personal turn: "Hic situs est Rufus, pulso qui Vindice quondam/imperium adseruit non sibi sed patriae." Plin. *ep.* 9.19.
178. *RIC.* I. 184 nr. 8.
    *RIC.*I. 184 nr. 1; cf. Brunt p.547ff. –
    *RIC.*I. 192 nr. 5; 6 –
    *RIC.*I. 184 nr. 9. 10; *ibid.* 185 11-13; 15, 16; *ibid.*186 nr. 28;*ibid.* 187 nr. 33-34 and 192 nr. 7 –
    *RIC.*I. 181 nr. 1-5; *ibid.* 183 nr. 22 and 185 nr. 17 –
    *RIC.*I. 184 nr. 2; *ibid.* 187 nr. 39.
    The MARS ADSERTOR and one of the MARS ULTOR coins are in the *RIC.* assigned to the coinage of Civilis, but cf. note 167.
179. Cf. Martin p 54 on the coins with the legends MARS ULTOR and GENIUS P.R:"*Ultor* (ist) hier allgemein als Rächer oder Bestrafer von Untaten zu verstehen. Nach dem Zeitpunkt dieser Prägung ... kann es sich ... hier .. nur um die von Nero begangenen Vergehen handeln. Von daher gesehen ist die Verbindung mit dem *Genius populi Romani* besonders verständlich, denn es war das römische Volk, an dem diese Untaten begangen wurden."
180. ADSERTOR LIBERTATIS: *RIC.* 192 nr. 4 (This coin is in the *RIC.* assigned to the coinage of Civilis, but cf. note 167).
    SALUS GENERIS HUMANI: *RIC.* 186 nr. 22.
    Note also that Vindex called upon Galba "ut *humano generi* assertorem ducemque accomodaret" Suet. *Galba* 9.2; the slogan soon came to be identified with Galba's cause: it appears, in Greek, in the edict of Tiberius Iulius Alexander issued on the 6 th. of July 68 AD (Chalon p.50), and in his coinage it is one of the most recurrent of the legends: Instinsky p.7-8. Later, Nero was called "hostem generis humani" (Plin. *NH.* 7.46) and Galba is, in Tacitus, said to have been elected by "consensus generis humani" (*Hist.* I.30,2; cf. Kraay 1949,138).

181. Plut. *Galba* 5; Suet. *Galba* 10; – Plut. *Galba* 6.4.–; Suet. *Nero* 57; Zonar. 11, 13 p.42, 10-20 D.
182. Cf. the table in Stylow p.211-13.
183. Kraay 1949 p.140.
184. Note also his speech to Piso: "...nec mea senectus conferre plus populo Romano possit quam bonum successorem ..." (Tac. *Hist.* I.16; cf. Plut. *Galba* 21) and his dying words: "Δρᾶτε, ἔιπεν, εἰ τοῦτο τῷ δήμῳ Ῥωμαίων ἄμεινόν ἐστι". Plut. *Galba* 27; Tacitus has "... ferirent si ita <e> re publica videretur" but knew other versions: *Hist* I. 41,2. Galba's partisan, Q Pomponius Rufus, later described the rebellion as "bello qu <od> imp. G<a>lba pro <re p(ublica)> gessit." ("The reading given appears to be certain...") *IRT* 537
185. The legend AUGUSTUS P.R is "very striking": *BMC.* I p.ccviii; according to Stylow the legend LIBERTAS P.R is unique (p.52); I have noted only one parallel to VICTORIA P.R: *RIC.* 5^{II}, 544 nr. 1032 (Carausius) – but there may be more.
186. There is a catalogue of the anonymous coinage in Martin p.69ff and also in Nicolas p.13o3ff. For the sake of convenience I here refer only to the pages and numbers in the *RIC*.
187. The last of the coins quoted is in the *RIC.* assigned to the "military" class; but cf. note 167.
188. "Doubtful" *RIC.* I. 185.
189. Cf. note 172.
190. Posthumous according to Mattingly, but cf. Kraay 1956 p.53.
191. The legend is according to the *RIC.* VICTORIA S, but the *BMC.* I p.350 nr. 232 and $Cohen^2$ nr. 316 only have VICTORIA – and so has the specimen in the *Cabinet de France.* I am indepted to Anne Kromann Balling at the *Royal Collection of Coins and Medals* for her help with this and other numismatic problems.
192. "...open to suspicion and require the confirmation of specimens beyond doubt." *RIC.* I. 223; cf., however, *BMC.*I p.383: "There is nothing serious to be urged against this coin, *a priori*, and genuine specimens, such as C. 83, probably exist.".
The *BMC.*I, 374,45 SECURITAS P.R is a hybrid: *rev.* type of Otho.
193. "Very doubtful" *RIC.* II.17.
194. The note expressing doubt as to this legend is cancelled in the list of *corrigenda RIC.* II p.xv.
195. The two last instances were issued by Titus: in his own short reign there is a sudden reemergence of that type of legend:

CONG TER ... S.C.	*RIC.* II.127 (legend doubtful)
GENIO P.R. S.C	*RIC.* II. 131 nr. 127.
GENI P.R. S.C.	*RIC.* II. 130 nr. 126.
SECURITAS P.R. S.C	*RIC.* II. 130 nr. 119, 138 nr. 172 (Domitianus)

then it seems utterly to disappear – to be reintroduced by Nerva along with other Galban slogans.
196. On Nero and Otho cf. Tac. *Hist.* I.13 and 78.2; Suet. *Otho* 7 and 10.2; Plut.

Otho 3. On Vitellius and Nero cf. Tac. *Hist.* II.71 and 95; Suet. *Vitellius* 11,2.
197. *RIC.* I. 212 nr. 124 –
    RIC. I. 214 nr. 145 –
    RIC. I. 216, 159: posthum. according to Mattingly, but cf. note 190.
198. *RIC.* I. 220 nr. 13-17.
199. *RIC.* I. 229 nr. 13; *ibid.* 231 nr. 9 –
    RIC. I. 229 nr. 15.
200. Kraay 1956 p.57.
201. For a full survey see the instructive lists in Stylow p.212-3: On Otho's Alexandrine ΕΛΕΥΘΕΡΙΑ coins: Stylow p.160 note 64.
202. Kraay 1978,52.
203. Strack I, 178: "Vom Jahre 72 ab ist der Göttin (*sc. Libertatis*) Name und Bild wieder von den Münzen verschwunden, die flavische Monarchie hatte ihre Macht begründet, bedurfte der lockenden Fiktion nicht mehr. Erst nach 24 jähriger Pause verkündet die LIBERTAS PUBLICA des Nerva nach Domitians Ermordung wieder den Beginn einer neuen Zeit." Similarly Stylow p.54; commenting on the same phenomenon, Wickert prudently adds: "Offiziell ist *Libertas* natürlich immer da ..." (col. 2084).
204. Vindex, in his edicts, called Nero Ahenobarbus (Suet. *Nero* 41), and Octavia, in her curse (249): "Nero insitivus, Domitio genitus patre" – but that would readily suggest itself to any Roman who wished to defame that emperor: cf. Suet. *Nero* 7; Tac. *Ann.* 12.41,3.
205. As to the charge of having set fire to the city, the rebels will have known to profit from it. There does not, however, seem to be any reference to these charges on the coins – if, indeed, that is not what the mysterious VOLKANUS ULTOR is meant to signify. Mattingly (*BMC.* I p. cxcv) argued it is a moneyer's coin; Martin p.55 is doubtful. Note the expiatory offerings to Volcanus recorded in Tac. *Ann.* 15.44 and on the Flavian *ara incendii Neroniani CIL.* 6.826.
206. For the reasons of discontent see Brunt, especially p. 554ff.–
    SPQR was apparently one of the main war-cries (cf. note 169 and 170): Vindex swore allegiance to that body :Zonar. 11,13 p.41,12-19 D; Verginius Rufus wished to submit the question of the throne to it: Dio 63.25,3; Galba styled himself its "legatus" (Suet. *Galba* 10 and Plut. *Galba* 5) and was eventually proclaimed emperor by soldiery, Senate and people: Plut. *Galba* 7.2. On the first of January A.D.69 the soldiers in Germany swore allegiance to the SPQR; "Id sacramentum inane visum" – and on the third they went over to Vitellius: Tac. *Hist.* 1.12; 55,4; 56,2 and 57; see also Plut. *Galba* 22,3.
    Piso, in Tacitus (*Hist.*1.30,2), likewise acknowledged that reality was different: "Si res publica et senatus et populus vacua nomina sunt, vestra, commilitiones, interest, ne imperatorem pessimi faciant."
207. Crawford nr. 393.
208. As argued by Béranger p.73; against Crawford p.733.
209. Crawford nr. 440; 513.1.
210. Wickert col. 2083 (with previous lit.); Kraay 1949 p. 142; Brunt p. 535; Nicols p.89ff. Martin (p.62-3) goes too far, however, when he argues further that the

influence of republican slogans and designs on this coinage was neglibible: his own list of parallels speaks against him. Note also the solemn formulas I. O. MAX. CAPITOLINUS and VESTA P.R. QUIRITIUM; on the former see *BMC.* I, cxcix; the formula *P.R. Quiritium* was, in a sense, as old as Rome: see for instance Livy's version of the fetial formula of a treaty, a declaration of war and a *devotio* (I.24.5 (bis), I.32.13 (three times) and VIII.9.7 (four times). I cannot believe that such *formulae* were chosen at random.

211. Crawford nr. 266; 270; 391; 392.
 Of the emperors only Claudius had issued coins with *Libertas* and *pilleus:* Stylow p.46.
212. Crawford nr. 498; 499; 500; 501 and 506; the legends are either LIBERTAS or LEIBERTAS.
213. *BMC.* I p. cxcl; Martin p. 63. For the fame of the Brutus coin see Crawford 741 note 11.
214. Buecheler and Nordmeyer saw the problem and toyed with the idea of attributing the play to Pomponius Secundus who thought highly of the Gracchi; Nordmeyer, however, thought better of it in view of the influence of Seneca on the style of the *Octavia* (p.284).
 The problem remains – even if it has been overlooked by recent editors (Ballaira and Whitman): (Nordmeyer discusses the praise of the Gracchi and Livius Drusus) "Apud nullum neque poetam neque scriptorem pedestrem eiusmodi iudicium inveni. Vide vel hominum alienorum a partibus optimatium iudicia de tribunis illis, Valerii Maximi, Flori II 2 (III 14). Lucanus autem una cum Catilina eos Ditis carcere dignos censet (VI. 793). Gracchorum genus, formam, eloquentiam etiam adversarii admirantur et laudant, tamen nemo eo usque progressus est, ut "pietate et fide claros, legibus acres" nominaret. Neque eiusmodi quidquam sumere poeta poterat e Senecae consolationis ad Marciam ... capite 16... Quo modo explicanda sit discrepantia illa, nescio" (p.315).
215. Livy I.56.8; on the *adsertor* and *vindex libertatis* motives cf. Ogilvie *ad* III 44-49.
216. On Galba and Πρόνοια/PROVIDENT S.C. cf. Plut. *Galba* 5.2 and *RIC.* I.216 nr. 164 (posthum. according to Mattingly, but cf. note 190); see furthermore the discussion in Chalon p.49ff of Πρόνοια in the edict of Tiberius Iulius Alexander; Epictetus (III.15.14) has a story of a person who lost faith in the workings of Providence when Galba was murdered; there are some excellent observations on Galba's *providentia* in Charlesworth 1936, 107-8 and 114ff.
217. On the meaning of these coins see Charlesworth 1936 p.126.
218. 232; 44ff; 139ff and 160ff; see also Schwabl col. 807.
219. 392ff; Leo's conjecture *premas* was anticipated by Bentley (marginal note in his copy of Gronovius' 1682 edition, British Library 686.f.8); cf. Hosius, *app. crit. ad loc.–*
 Few will agree with Zwierlein 1966 in regarding this monologue as an example of "Überhandnehmen der Monologe" (p.119); neither is it, as it will appear, "unversehens" (id. p.123[8]) that Seneca begins to speak of Saturn: see, for instance, Schwabl, who rightly speaks of "die ungeheuerlich steigernde

Funktion des Zeitaltermythos im Drama ... Auf diese Weise erscheint Nero hier .. als halbapokalyptische Figur und der Zeitaltermythos mit seinen apokalyptischen Aspekten als das eigentlich sinngebende Element des Dramas" (Schwabl col. 807).

220. "The "Regeneration of Rome" was evidently one of the main war-cries" *BMC.* I cxciii:

Anonymous coinage	Galba
RIC. I 182 nr. 17 D; 18 Au	200 nr. 13 Au; 14 D; 15 Au; 16 D; 208 nr. 87 Au; 88 D.
RIC. I 182 nr. 19 D.	200 nr. 17 Au; 18 D.
RIC. I	208 nr. 89 Au; 90 D; 210 nr. 113 Au, 114 D; 211 nr. 121 D.

221. He records Agrippina's *damnatio memoriae* 609ff: cf Nordmeyer 273ff. (As for Acte's "monument" 196ff I prefer the interpretation of Herington 1977 p.276 to Ladek's widely accepted one)
There are 1) verbal quotations from official Claudian propaganda and 2) for polemical purposes, from Nero's:
1. "ultra Oceanum" (27);
cf. *ILS* 212 (Claudius' speach in Lyon): "insolentior esse videar et quaesisse iactationem gloriae prolati imperi ultra Oceanum"; Sen. *Apocol.* 12.26-7 "ultra noti/litora ponti" and also the expressions "Oceanus ... ultra" and "citra.. Oceanum" in the poems (*Anth. lat.* 419.3; 423.4) which in celebrating Claudius' conquest of Britain clearly reflect official slogans and propaganda (Nordmeyer 311 note 1).
– "primus" (41);
cf. *ILS* 216 (inscription on Claudius' triumphal arch in Rome) "primus in dici[onem...".
– "iugum" (41) and "ignoti" (29) also occur in the poems mentioned above (*Anth.lat.* 426.8 and 424.3).
2. The symbols of the Golden Age and the sheathed sword are, as we have seen, turned against him; there are revealing quotations from the *De clementia:* "ego ... patiar ...?" (I.9,4 Augustus) and 462 "An patiar ...?" (Nero) and Nero mocks the political ideals which his tutor (and his own coins) had advertised: *clementia* (442): *dementia* (496) and puts his own instead: he shall not *servare* (490), but Rome and the Senate shall *servire* (492). In his hatred for the people he does, however, reproach them for being ungrateful for his *clementia* and *pax* (835-6). See also Hosius *ad* 437bff.
222. On Vespasian's attitude towards Nero and Claudius see for instance Charlesworth 1937 p.54. Titus had been educated with Britannicus and later paid homage to his memory: Suet. *Tit.* 2; cf. *BMC.* II p.293 nr. 306. On Vespasian and Galba see Gagé.
223. Sil. *Pun.* 3. 571ff: one of the ways it could be done.
224. Tac. *Hist.* IV.42.6 (K. Wellesly).
Ladek 1891 p.94 questioned Meiser's date: 69-70 (p.18) as giving the author

too little time and tranquillity to write; the argument is not cogent: consider, for instance, Cicero's output in 44-43 BC.
225. Tac. *Hist.* I.16.
226. On the exiled nobility: 89; 242; 437bff; 467ff; on Vindex and the exiles see Joann. Antioch. fr. 91 Muell. v. 6-10; at his first declaration against Nero Galba deplored their fate: "Igitur cum ... conscendisset tribunal, propositis ante se damnatorum occisorumque a Nerone quam plurimis imaginibus et astante nobili puero, quem exulantem e proxima Baliari insula ob id ipsum acciverat, deploravit temporum statum ..." (Suet. *Galba* 10; cf. Plut. *Galba* 5). Tacitus testifies to the importance of the exiles' following at Rome: "Pars populi integra et magnis domibus adnexa, clientes libertique damnatorum et exulum in spem erecti" (*sc.* at the death of Nero) (*Hist.* 1.4,3). Galba recalled them, but failed to satisfy their needs: Tac. *Hist.* 2.92; among them were Piso and Helvidius Priscus: *ibid.* 1.48 and 4.6; the former he adopted, the latter arranged his funeral: Plut. *Galba* 28.3. Some of these nobles probably belonged to, or had connections with, the so-called "stoic opposition": Helvidius Priscus is a well known example; note also that Laco and Piso originally had met at Rubellius Plautus' house (Tac.*Hist.* 1.14); this author records the execution of that stoic noble (437b ff) and presents *Seneca* as his (and Octavia's) heroic defendant.
227. Paul. Fest. p.249 (Lindsay); there is a discussion of the evidence in Helm 1954 col. 1569ff; Pedroli p.9ff and in Hermann.
228. The very subjects: Roman victory at Clastidium, Ambracia and Pydna, the heroism of Decius and the establishment of the republic – speak for themselves; see also the fragments of Accius' *Decius* IV and of his *Brutus* II.8ff and IV (*TRF*); Cicero's *pro Sestio* 58.123 and the *scholia ad loc.* testify to the readiness of that audience to respond to a play's political message; cf Hermann p.144 and 148 ff.
229. Accius' *Brutus* – probably written for D. Iunius Brutus – and the *Brutus* written by a menber of the *gens Cassia* (Varro *Ling.* 6.7) – or is *Cassi* a scribal error for *L.Acci* (Pedroli 15)?
Arguing from *Octavia* and from Maternus' *Cato* and *Domitius* P.L. Schmidt, I (also *Der kleine Pauly* 4 col. 1113-14) suggests that they should not be described as *praetextae*, in the republican sense of the word, but rather as tragedies. The argument presupposes that Maternus' *Domitius* dealt with the republican martyr of that name – which is far from being certain: Helm 1954 col. 1574; and can it be taken for granted that Maternus' *Cato* expressed a tragic sentiment comparable to Lucan's "Victrix causa dis placuit, sed victa Catoni"? Maternus had, after all, seen the fall of the once victorious dynasty.
230. The testimony is collected in Bollinger p.30ff; see also Hermann p.152ff and MacMullen p.170ff.
231. Tac. *Dial.* 3,4: the titles were *Cato* and *Domitius*. I disregard the praetexta *Vescio* (?) of Persius, the subject of which is unknown. Of Pomponius Secundus' *Aeneas* little is known – not even the title is certain. The testimony suggests little more than, perhaps, "a Silver Latin fashion for historical plays" Herington 1961 p.28.

232. Tac. *Dial.* 11.3: the text is uncertain. In Tac.*Hist.* 1.37,5 Polyclitus, Vatinius and Aegialus are spoken of as dead; Polyclitus was executed on Galba's orders (Plut. *Galba* 17), of an Aegialus nothing is known (*Helius?* Lips.). Whoever he was, the context suggests that he and Vatinius were executed (for crimes which, according to Otho, were far less serious than those of Galba's freedman, Icelus): Vater p.579. Granted that Maternus' play did deal with Vatinius (differently Vater p.581ff – *et alii alia*) it would surely have to belong to Galba's rather than Nero's reign: against Gudeman[2] *ad loc.* – but not, it seems, for any good reasons.
233. Tac. *Dial.* 2; 3.3; "auditoriis et theatris": 10.5.
234. Herington 1961 p.25 (arguing from Accius' *Brutus* and the curious *praetexta* of Balbus). Contra: Bruckner p. 140[4] – and Herington did perhaps overstate his case, but the alternative, that our author should be responsible for this bold innovation does not recommend itself: the very ease with which he handles the tripartition speaks against it.
235. Accius, *Brutus* I and II (*TRF*); Mickwitz p.241 does not, in my view, prove that Poppaea's dream was modelled directly on that of Tarquin.
236. The *didascalia* is quoted in Klotz, *Scaen. Rom. Frag.* I p.309.
237. Cf. note 181.
238. Plut. *Galba* 8.5; Tac. *Hist.* I.78,2 and Suet. *Otho* 7.
239. Zonar. 11,14 p.43, 19-25 D; Octavia will in all likelihood have been among those who received these posthumous honours.
240. *ILS* 238: "... signum Libertatis restitutae Ser. Galbae imperatoris Aug..." (from the 15th October AD 68).
241. Plut. *Galba* 17.4; cf. Tac. *Hist.* I.72,3.
242. Syme p.670-1.
243. Cf. P.L. Schmidt, III.
244. Yavetz p.124.
245. Suet. *Nero* 57.
246. Likewise Bruckner 145 note 19 (with a full discussion); Zwierlein vacillates: in 1976 p.182 he refers to 387b-388a as "sicher unecht", but in 1979 p.180 note 60 he prefers Ritter's solution – but has some doubts whether the problem should be solved in this way at all.
247. The symmetrical structure of this speech (10×10) makes Fuchs' suggestion of a lacuna between 486 and 487 singularly unattractive (p.75).
248. Fuchs (p.75) and Ageno argue in favour of a lacuna after 518 or 517.
249. Without going into the numerical aspects P.L. Schmidt, III has arrived at a partition of this scene which also stresses the mediative function of Nero's declaration: 437b – 531 and 532 – 591; cf. Bruckner p.40ff and 91ff.
250. Herrmann 1924 (p.169) and Ballaira (p.II) suggest that the fifth episode (or midday of the second (?) day: Fuchs p.72) begins in 820. The symmetrical structure of 780-845 ($26 \cdot 14 \cdot 26$) does not, however, conform at all well with such a division.
251. Leo 513.
252. Cf. however Zwierlein 1966 p.73[3]: "Nur in *Oct.* 273 ("Quae fama modo venit

ad aures?") gibt der Chor eine gewisse Motivierung seines Auftretens; aber dieses Stück stammt nicht von Seneca."
253. Fuchs p.72.
254. Marek p.43; Stoessl coll. 2429; Fuchs p.72; Runchina p.70.
255. Zwierlein 1966 p.44.
256. Münscher[b] p.210.
257. The evidence is ambiguous; various explanations have been suggested: see for instance Ballaira *ad* 729.
258. Vespasian at first defamed Vitellius and championed Otho. Later both were ignominuously ignored: Ferrill 268ff.
259. Galba was thought, however, to have had certain reservations: "Credo et rei publicae curam subisse, frustra a Nerone translatae si apud Othonem relinqueretur" – Tacitus (*Hist.* I.13,2) on Galba's unwillingness to adopt Otho.
260. Tac. *Hist.* I.78,2.
261. Likewise T.D. Barnes in a paper on "The Date of the *Octavia*" (*MH* 39, 1982, 215ff) which reached me when reading the final proofs. He further convincingly argues: "A dramatist writing while Tigellinus retained influence had an obvious motive for leaving Nero's prefect (*sc.* in the play) anonymous." and concludes: "If the date of the *Octavia* is not to be left imprecise, then the reign of Galba is surely the most appropriate historical context for its composition." (p. 217).